LET'S START OVER

DAVID G. McKECHNIE

Owen
God bless you!
Love,
Dave
'93

God did not give us the secret of how to begin things for that is God's secret kept from the creation. But the secret God gave to us is how to begin again.

OLD JEWISH PROVERB

To Betty McKechnie,

My mother, my mentor and the greatest example of Christian hospitality I know.

CONTENTS

Introduction

ACKNOWLEDGEMENTS

Many people have helped me begin again with relationships and problems. To begin again with every situation is tangible proof that God's grace is always greater than my need.

The following people have given me a boost to complete this book. I am thankful to the congregation and elders of Grace Presbyterian Church, Houston, for encouraging me to put these ideas in print. My wife, Linda and children, Peter and Sheri, kept affirming that I had something to say to a wider audience. Lisa Schwartz honestly and patiently edited. Jim Lamar and Sheila Liu helped research sources. Charlotte Flader, my Administrative Assistant, diligently fired material into her word processor and put it in acceptable condition for the publisher. Linda and Sam Bradshaw graciously opened their lovely Lake Travis home for several days of undisturbed editing before I let go of the manuscript. In the serenity of that setting, overlooking the blue, green water, I found peace with this effort.

Thanks to these special people in my life. What a gift! If this book helps someone—to God be the glory!

David G. McKechnie

INTRODUCTION

As a pastor, I hear it week after week. Many people do not believe they can start over. People insist that their problem is so overwhelming that there is absolutely nothing they can do about it. I believe in the power of God. I believe that Ezekiel meant it when he said "Get yourselves a new heart and a new spirit." Ezekiel 18:31.

The purpose of this book is to provide inspiration for you to start over. Along with the inspiration are some tools. However, more important than any insights I might provide, is your attitude. You can allow your mind to absorb the energy of God's spirit. You can start over.

I do not believe that your age, your background, your education, or your failures have anything to do with the future. You can start all over again by God's grace.

Inside of you is tremendous power. Your resilience can be a source of strength to others. You can believe in the power to change. That is one of the promises extended to us through Jesus Christ.

How do you keep the momentum going? In numerous places, I have attempted to help you move beyond the initial burst of enthusiasm to make change happen. How to keep a new start going. That is our task.

As you read the following twelve chapters, you will experience the stories of those who have successfully started over. These stories will renew your own energy and confidence. The authority of the Bible is real. Immerse yourself in that and pray and I believe you will experience a power to start over.

By reading this far, you have resisted tripping over the initial step. Therefore, my friend, walk on.

God bless you!

David G. McKechnie
Houston, Texas
Summer, 1993

CHAPTER ONE

Starting Over With Your Past

II Corinthians 3:12-18

The knife neatly sliced open the envelope. It was a letter from another Presbyterian pastor. It was an apology. He simply copied an item I had written for our church newsletter entitled, "To The Family Of Grace."

His letter said, "I was up against a publishing deadline, Dave. I needed something and I simply took it, changed a few words and put my name on it and let it go."

Guilt overwhelmed him. He wrote to apologize and say he was sorry. I had not seen the item in his newsletter. It really did not bother me. But it sure bothered him! He said, "I want to start our relationship all over again." Starting over. What a wonderful opportunity!

Jogging is not enjoyable for me. I do it anyway. I do it for my health. Three or four mornings a week, I run at 6 a.m. January 1-10 always intrigues me. There are

1

plenty of new faces in the neighborhood out there at 6 a.m. They are all trying to fulfill New Year's Resolutions. "I'm going to get in shape." "I'm going to lose twenty pounds!" All of them have good intentions. They are starting over. But you can count on it, by March most of the "resolvers" have dropped out of the fitness race and reverted back to the same old routine. Starting over is tough! It requires physical and mental toughness.

George Bernard Shaw was asked if he could live his life over as any character out of history—who would it be? Shaw reacted, "I would choose to be the man George Bernard Shaw could have been but never was."

I stood captivated by the 58,132 names grit-blasted into black granite at the Vietnam Veteran's Memorial in Washington, D.C. Each name a life. Flowers, messages, photos, tears and tracings sobered me. Because one day my name will be carved in granite. Death is the biggest bully on the block of life.

Before death, God gives us the grace to look reality in the eye and stare it down. The past is not determinative. God is for us. "The mercy of the Lord is from everlasting to everlasting." The resurrection of Jesus Christ makes all the difference in the world. It is God's refusal to give up on you and me. Hope is alive!

A high school principal, the first week in January, wiped out all of the detentions the students had accumulated from September through December. Why? Because he wanted them to have the opportunity to start over.

Tuesdays I try to reserve for writing sermons. Sure that well-intentioned disciplined schedule gets interrupted. However, if I can get my thoughts on paper by

Tuesday, I am less anxious as I carry out my responsibilities building to Sundays.

Occasionally, I do not have a good feeling by 5 p.m. on Tuesday. Somehow, the sermon just will not jell. Thursdays I try to preserve for myself. My day off. But, when the sermon I wrote on Tuesday falls short of my expectations, I often end up starting over on Thursday. At least I gain some peace of mind even if it is at the expense of my day off. Starting over is such a wonderful gift!

Moses had just come down off Mount Sinai with the Ten Commandments in his hands. He had been in the very presence of God to receive that truth. His face shone with the splendor of God. He reflected something of God's beauty, brightness and glory. But his face was so bright that people pulled back from him. They were afraid of him. Yet, it was an opportunity for the people of God to start over. After Moses had addressed the people, he put a veil over his face so they would not see the splendor fade.

That is the picture that is in the mind of the Apostle Paul as he writes this letter to that little, dusty group of Christians in Corinth. He sees the old covenant, the old relationship between God and humankind, as fading. The law did not do the job. They could not fulfill all of the law's demands. The law appeared to them as a barrier over which they could not climb to get back into right relationship with God.

Paul affirms the new covenant, a new relationship between God and humankind that is complete, dazzling, stunning, bright and perfect. An opportunity to start over. It is God's love revealed in Jesus Christ, the full

3

and final revelation of his Grace. The magnetic pull of the mercy of God.

Paul turns on his Jewish friends and attacks, "You live with a veil over your face. The Old Testament should be pointing you to Jesus Christ as the Messiah. Instead of that, you have a veil over your face. It is hiding the glory of Jesus Christ, the brightness of the light of Christ from you. You are missing it!" Paul's laser of truth turns to us. "You do not have a veil over your face. You can see clearly and accurately God's love in Jesus Christ."

Do you remember the Broadway show "On A Clear Day You Can See Forever?" If you have ever climbed in the Rockies or the Alps, and the sky is blue, no clouds, you really sense that on a clear day it feels like you can see forever. Paul says, it is not just your vision that is back in focus in terms of a Savior, but you are to reflect God's glory. Your face, your life, ought to reflect something of God's glory. And one of the ways it happens is when you grow into a "likeness" of Christ. One of the ways we show that "likeness" of Christ is through forgiveness. Perhaps forgiveness of ourselves or of others.

All of us want to reach back into our past and eradicate some painful moment or memory. None of us are free from wanting to reach back into our history and excise an experience that has tainted our lives. Maybe somebody lied to us. Maybe we lied to somebody. Maybe we ignored somebody's call for help. Maybe somebody ignored our call for help. Maybe somebody abused us. Maybe we abused somebody else. Maybe we cheated. Maybe somebody cheated on us. All of us want to reach back into our memories and surgically remove some cancerous memory.

Lewis Smedes wrote, "The only power that can stop the inexorable stream of painful memories is the faculty of forgiveness." Is forgiveness really God's invention? Forgiveness is God's invention to help us deal with the pain and the hurt that we impose on each other in this world. It is not only God's invention but also, God's gift to us. God began with forgiveness. God invites us to taste the sweet joy of forgiveness in our lives. Better still, it is ours to take and apply. Even though you hurt other people deeply, even though you are unfair to yourself and to others, even though you know your need for forgiveness, you find it difficult to accept and apply.

The pastor stopped by the farmhouse to visit. His member was gently rockin' in his chair on the porch. The farmer's dog kept whining throughout the visit. Finally the pastor asked, "Why does your dog keep on whining?" The old gentleman replied, "She's lying on a nail and it only hurts her enough to whine, but not enough to move!"

Authentic Christianity calls us not to whine, but to move. For forgiveness to work, somebody has to quit whining and start moving!

Why is forgiveness so difficult? What love's toughest task? Forgiveness. What is love's greatest risk? Forgiveness. There is something unfair, awkward and unnatural about forgiveness. We have an inclination, an innate sense that says, "Hey, somebody does you wrong, they better be punished! They deserve it! They ought to get it back! It's only natural!" But, the power of God's

5

love in Jesus Christ says, "No, the natural rules can be broken."

Better than seventy-five years ago, fire destroyed Thomas Edison's factory in New Jersey. The damage exceeded two million dollars. Much of his life's work went up in smoke that December night. The following day, Thomas Edison reviewed the ruins and said, "There is great value in disaster. All our mistakes are burned up. Thank God we can start anew."

In a small community just north of the city of Houston, someone had a vision of the Virgin Mary and some saw a vision of Jesus. It looked to me like it was in a junkyard. All of the media accounts drew crowds. All I saw was some kind of reflection. No Virgin Mary. No vision of Jesus. What I do know is some people thought it was real. They saw something spiritual or something enlightening in all of that. In a matter of days, all the hype disappeared as did the accounts of visions.

A young woman in the Philippines insisted that she had visions of Jesus. Her priest sent her to her Bishop. The Bishop visited with her and suggested, "My daughter, the next time you have a vision of Jesus, talk with Jesus and ask him what sin it was that I committed as your Bishop when I was just a young priest? And be sure and come back and tell me about it."

The Bishop knew that only he remembered the sin and he had told it to his confessor and to Jesus Christ. He felt safe. Several months later, she came back and surprised him. "Bishop, I have had a vision of Jesus." He said, "Good, tell me about it. Did you ask him about me?" And she said, "Yes, I did." "Well," he said, "What did he say?" He said, "I have forgotten."

Starting Over With Your Past

Angela and David showed up for a premarital interview. My normal opener is, "How did you meet?" When they told me they had met at a drug rehabilitation center, I was intrigued. Obviously, there was more to the story. There was. Indeed, there was much more.

David had received a head injury while working offshore on a drilling rig. The injury left him with the loss of an eye. He had received substantial compensation for the damage sustained. With his new found affluence and time on his hands, he became involved with cocaine and it consumed him.

Angela came to the rehabilitation center because of her dependency on alcohol. Both found each other in the rehabilitation program. They were determined to start over.

God's grace in Jesus Christ changed their lives. They are ready to establish a relationship on a biblical foundation. They love to tell people about the mercy of Jesus Christ that enabled them to start over.

My friend, there is a "Divine Amnesia" that washes over you. It is a measure of God's mercy. That "Divine Amnesia" releases a cleansing power that can give you a new perspective on life.

Cartoonists often make us smile by depicting people walking under a dark cloud. We expect the worst for them. You do not have to walk forever under a black cloud of personal shame. You do not have to set your feet in wet cement in anticipation of that cement hardening into self-accusation. God wants to release you from the terror of your sins. You can turn things around. You can reverse your field just like a running back. He instinctively knows he better reverse the field if he is going to find any openings at all to run for daylight. Moses reversed his field. Jonah, Rahab, Elijah, Peter, Paul, they all reversed their fields. That is one of God's gifts to you. Forgiveness is God's invention. God's way for you to start over.

Curtis Johnson, a member of my congregation, told me that his father was in the construction business. His father observed that a skilsaw had disappeared from the company box.

He gathered all of the employees together. He said, "If the skilsaw does not appear tomorrow, I will deduct the price of the skilsaw from everybody's paycheck next Friday." Curtis tells me that the next day, eight skilsaws appeared. Business started over the next day on a different basis.

All of us fail at different times in life. But remember, failure is not fatal. When the soldiers drove the nails into that rough Roman cross through the hands of Jesus, it appeared that the crucifixion was a tremendous failure. It turned out to be the supreme expression of compassion and the turning point in history.

Henry Ford's philosophy was, "Failure is not failure but the opportunity to begin again...more intelligently."

Failure can make you bitter or it can make you better. Those negative thoughts do far more damage to us personally than they do to anyone else. A wise person acknowledges the power of word and thoughts. Someone said, "Acid can do more harm to the vessel in which it is stored, than the object on which it is poured."

Failure is painful. The best remedy is to start over. Pick up the pieces. Repent. Make the necessary restitution and apologies. Accept the power of Christ's forgiveness and begin again cognizant of the grace of Christ that urges you to do it.

When we need to start over, we usually hesitate, stammer and stew. Worry overwhelms us. Our hesitancy paralyzes us. Worry, literally translated is, "to strangle." The path of least resistance for us is to strangle a good idea. God calls for our response. God's grace is extended to us. "For my power is made perfect in weakness." II Corinthians 12:9.

John Calvin used to walk around Geneva with one of those floppy, big, black hats. When you visit the great Reformed Cathedral in Geneva, you can see Calvin's chair. It was from that chair in "Calvin's Auditorium" that he dispensed his knowledge to the citizens of Geneva at 7 a.m. each day.

He taught that, within us, there is that which deserves the hatred of God. "God, who is perfect righteousness, cannot love the iniquity which he sees in all. All of us, therefore, have that within us which deserves the hatred of God." (Institutes of the Christian Religion, 1536) We know that. We do not have to be told that. We sense that. But, by God's grace, we can reverse the field and start all over again.

Oh, I know. Hurts are real. They are painful. They are deep. They are so unfair. Surely you fail to understand what this person did to me? Surely you understand the burden that I carry for what I did? Yes, it hurts. Those deep tears in the fiber of human relationships are costly. The cost is enormous. I not only hurt, but I hate! I really hate, at times. That malice can rob you of the ability to even think about a conversation with someone that has wronged you or someone you have wronged.

Let's Start Over

That malice can temporarily paralyze any muscle you might attempt to use when it comes to writing a little note to try to set things right. Hurt and hate are a volatile mix.

But, there is forgiveness. There is power in forgiveness beyond any understanding of the word itself. We can turn back the flow of pain. We can be released from those memories that terrorize us. But remember, my friends, forgiveness is not a feeling. Forgiveness is always a choice. You choose to forgive. You choose to deprive yourself and others of the healing offered in God's invention of forgiveness. Forgiveness in Jesus Christ reverses the corrosive action of our sins. We can start over. That is Paul's point in II Corinthians 5:17, "Therefore, if anyone is in Christ, he is a new creation, the old is passed away." The new—the new, has begun.

In ancient Greece, when someone was wronged, the statement would be written out and then taken outside and nailed to a post. A nail was driven through the written charges. When it was nailed to the post, it meant the issue was settled. It was done. It was over. It was posted for all the world to know. It was made public. That was exoneration.

What hurt is it that you insist on carrying? Jesus Christ invites you to nail it to the cross. When you nail it to the cross, you release an energy, a love, a power that exonerates because of the cross of Jesus Christ. It floods the tissue of your memory expunging those hurts, those sins that you have so carefully harbored. Your pain and the pain you have imposed on others has an antidote in the cross of Jesus Christ. Those sins that you have hoarded so dangerously no longer need to control

10

you. Forgiveness is not simply said. Words must be put into action. Forgiveness must be done.

When our son, Peter, was in first grade, one of the very important events to him was the school carnival. This was a big deal! All parents were solicited for contributions of time, cookies, money, and ideas. Linda did her fair share.

When the day of the carnival finally arrived, Linda, Peter and I traipsed down to the school. After all, we were good parents. My attitude was condescending. When we arrived, we noticed there was a tremendous amount of trash all around, and numerous people leaving. Some were dismantling the booths.

It was very obvious that we had misjudged the time of the carnival. Linda made a mistake. Peter was frustrated, disappointed, and angry. Linda did her best to apologize. She, too, was upset. With all the emotion that a first-grader could generate, Peter spontaneously hugged his mother and said, "It's O.K., Mom."

There is joy in starting over!

Wally "Famous" Amos soared to success with his chocolate chip cookies. His story exemplifies the necessity of starting over with your past. With no experience or security, Wally boldly promoted his first-class cookies with their first-class ingredients. He felt there was room at the top for that kind of quality. He took the plunge. No matter where you travel, Wally's chocolate chip cookies are there.

I am an early riser. I enjoy getting up early and cherishing the early quietness. Saturday morning is no exception. When the children were growing up, I loved to get up early, jog, read the paper and prepare breakfast. While everyone was still sleeping, I would go to the kitchen and mix my famous batter. I would set the table, pour the juice and get out the real Canadian maple syrup. By about 9 a.m., the grill was perfect and I was ready. I would begin to call for everyone to come to the table. Slowly but reluctantly, Linda, Peter and Sheri would stagger to the breakfast table. They ate it, but not with the enthusiasm I would have cherished.

After many years of this practice, when Peter and Sheri were teenagers, they finally made an announcement to me one Saturday morning. They obviously resented getting up on Saturday morning. They told me they hated pancakes. They did not like my real Canadian maple syrup. They did not like me hollering. That was tough medicine for me to swallow! All these years, I thought I was doing the family a great service. They took the risk of telling me the truth. I needed their forgiveness.

Now, Saturday mornings are very quiet at my house. I proceed with my routine. I allow them to enjoy their rest.

Every step of faith demands risk. Starting over demands risk. The anonymous author of the following poem has captured the essence of starting over—testing yourself, reaching out, pushing your limits, trying new things, standing up for your faith and accepting challenges.

> *To laugh*
> *is to risk appearing the fool.*
> *To weep*
> *is to risk appearing sentimental.*

Starting Over With Your Past

To reach out for another
is to risk involvement.
To expose feelings
is to risk exposing your true self.
To place your ideas, your dreams, before the crowd
is to risk loss.
To love
is to risk not being loved in return.
To live
is to risk dying.
To hope
is to risk despair.
To go forward in
the face of overwhelming odds is to risk
failure.
But risk we must.
Because the greatest hazard in life
is to risk nothing.
The person who risks nothing does nothing, has
nothing, is nothing.
He may avoid suffering and sorrow, but he cannot
learn, feel change, grow or love.
Chained by his certitudes, he is a slave.
He has forfeited his freedom.
Only a person who risks is free.

To start over, you need a supportive community. I have found that in the church of Jesus Christ. How do you start over with your church?

CHAPTER TWO

Starting Over With Your Church

Ephesians 3:14-21

Tommy Heinsohn was a great basketball player for the Boston Celtics. Later in his career, he coached the Boston Celtics. Tommy published a book, *Give 'Em The Hook.* He gives us a fascinating inside look at pro sports, "I believe the need that motivates most great athletes is some form of love-deprivation." He defines that, "I call it the love-ache." Then he goes on to talk about Larry Bird. Larry Bird was one of the best practitioners of basketball.

"Larry Bird is as compelled, as obsessed and as driven as any athlete I have ever seen." Then he added, "There has to be some of this love-ache in him." If you know the Larry Bird story, you know that his father was an alcoholic. His father, defeated by alcohol, committed suicide. Yes, I think Heinsohn is right. There is some love-ache in Larry Bird. Yes, there is some love-ache in all the great athletes. But they are not alone. I have news for Heinsohn. The news is that we all have some of that love-ache in us.

Presidents Reagan and Clinton are children of alcoholics. They know something of that love-ache.

That love-ache is a spiritual disease that literally cripples you. You have some of that love-ache. There really is something broken in you that money, sex, power, or status cannot fix. So you traipse through life with your facade. You look so good; you have all the trappings. You appear to have it all together or so you would have people think. Then you have a tragedy, a murder, a suicide, a divorce, a bankruptcy or a loss of any kind. It is like a poisoned gas, this love-ache. It penetrates to every corner in our lives. Crazy, isn't it?

Crazy. Because we have so much. But why do we hurt so? We have so much. Why don't we feel fulfilled? We have health, education, security, position and power. Why don't we have any sense of worth? We go off compulsively, in all directions, trying to get recognition, trying to get acceptance, trying to get affirmation. That love-ache is in all of us.

An elementary school student was told to list some verbs in the present tense. Then she was told to put these verbs in the perfect tense. One of the verbs she was given was live. She thought, chewed her pencil and finally responded, "I don't know what live is in the perfect tense. It has to be love." Grammatically, she was wrong; philosophically, she was right. The perfect tense of live, I guess, really is love.

Charles Colson struck home for me when he said, "All the kings of history sent their people out to die for them. Jesus was the only king that went out to die for his people."

The love of Christ—what a delightful surprise!

Paul sensed human need when he wrote Ephesians 3. He knew there was love-ache. Someone described Ephesians 3 as really "theology on its knees." How descriptive! For Paul says, "I bow my knees to the Father...and I pray that you might be strengthened in the inner man."

What is he talking about, the "inner man?" Is there a little person running around inside of us? No. He is talking about a Greek phrase. "Inner man." The Greek phrase "inner man" refers to reason, conscience and will. Paul is explaining how the love of Christ can impact our inner being; our reason distinguishes between right and wrong. Further, we have the wisdom to make good decisions. The love of Christ can sensitize the conscience to the needs that surround us. Sensitizing us to the presence of God at work in our lives is an action of the Holy Spirit. But, it is not all God's job. God created us with knowledge, will and emotions. Exercising the will is our prerogative. The will to carry through on our good intentions to some redemptive end is our agenda. Paul knew that we were a unique species; that we have the best mind; that we have the best method of communication; that we have the very best handling gear. Our hands are unique instruments. By chance or by design? Paul saw it as by design. So, he prays for his Church, prays for all of us as members of the body of Christ that we might be strengthened in the inner man. Strengthened in terms of reason, conscience and will.

Thoreau, in Walden said, "The mass of men lead lives of quiet desperation, and some of it not so quiet." The wealthiest man in Texas is a Presbyterian. His name is Ross Perot. He was an IBM sales representative. At IBM, he was very successful. In one year he realized the maximum annual compensation allowed by IBM by January 19. That was in 1962. He saw in the computer market a niche for customized software. When IBM was cool to the idea, Perot's frustration grew.

While waiting in a Dallas barbershop, he thumbed through a *Reader's Digest* and discovered Thoreau's quote: "The mass of men lead lives of quiet desperation." Inspired, on the spot he decided to leave the IBM womb and start Electronic Data Systems. It was the sale of E.D.S. to General Motors that enabled Perot to corral massive wealth. Today, Perot is still a political force. Thoreau's thoughtful statement triggered his love-ache into action. Thoreau understood the love-ache. Heinsohn understands the love-ache, but so do you. So do I.

Paul talks in geometric terms of the love of God in Jesus Christ. He talks about its height, and then its depth. What does he mean by talking about the arms of Jesus Christ stretching for everyone everywhere in the world, at all times, at all places and all ages? That love is so deep that God allowed his son to experience death on our behalf. The length to which God would go on our behalf is to allow his son a demeaning death on a Roman cross. That is the vastness of God's love in Jesus Christ. How do we explain that? How do we measure that? We only kneel in gratitude before that cross. We

17

only rise from our knees and live out our gratitude because of that cross.

The Eiffel Tower just had its 104th birthday. Have you every seen that monument? Enormous! It was built to celebrate the centennial of the French Revolution. Dedicated in 1889, the Eiffel embodies the elegant flair of the capital of France. Somebody figured out that if the Eiffel Tower could represent the age of this world, the amount of time that humankind has shared life on this planet is the thickness of the thin skin of paint at the top of the pinnacle of that little ball on the peak of the Eiffel Tower. That is the amount of time we have had an impact on this planet and its residents.

When I heard that, I thought about the church of Jesus Christ. We need the insights, the experience and the perception of all of us to gain some appreciation of how comprehensive God's love is. No one is outside of that love. There is no place you can hide adequately from that love.

Where can you experience that love? In the church. Am I talking about architecture? Am I talking about Notre Dame in Paris? St. Paul's in London? St. Peter's in Rome? The National Cathedral in Washington? St. Giles' in Edinburgh? No! I am talking about a community of faith, a forgiven community and a community that forgives. There is a little ditty that kids sing about the church; that the church is not a steeple, the church is a people.

That is the truth. You realize that the church is the one place where we are all equal. It is the only place where we are equal. We are just a bunch of sinners in need of God's grace. I don't care about the extent of your affluence. I don't care about the extent of your status. I don't care about the extent of your roots. The only characteristic that draws us together is our need for God's grace in Jesus Christ. We are not equal in terms of education. We certainly are not equal before our bankers. We are not equal on the tennis court. We are not equal in the shopping centers. We are not equal in the corporate structure. Only in the church of Jesus Christ do we have common ground. It is based on the love-ache in all of us.

Wall Street knows John Templeton as an astute money manager. The Templeton Fund has some fourteen billion dollars in assets. Religious leaders around the world know him as a devout man who annually awards a large cash prize to recognize "Progress in Religion."

The Templeton Prize has a higher monetary value than the Nobel Prize. The purse is usually in the range of four hundred and fifty thousand dollars. Says Templeton; "Alfred Nobel had a blind spot. He omitted the most important area where growth is needed— spirituality."

In the TV series "MASH", a raw, young teenage recruit was on sentry duty during a heavy bombing raid. He was shaking in his boots. He ran into the bombastic Colonel Potter. The compassionate colonel turned to him and said, "Afraid, son?" "NNNNNo, jjjust nervous." He lied. He stammered out his response. The old colonel looked at him and said, "Oh, if you had any brains at all, you'd be scared to death."

You know, if we had any brains at all, we would be scared to death to go it alone in this world. Scared to death to go without the community of faith. Scared to death to go without participating in the church of Jesus Christ. Love is best known not by isolated contemplation or by climbing up into some cave with a guru somewhere. Love is best known in community. John Wesley, the man who is credited with founding the Methodist Church, used to love to say, "God knows nothing of solitary religion."

Okay, then how do you start over with the church? Overlook the abuses and the mistakes of the church—the things that have been done in the name of Christ that are a detriment to the redemptive cause. There are plenty of abuses. I have made plenty of mistakes. You have made plenty of mistakes. Together, we have made plenty of mistakes. But if you are going to start over with the church, you have to overlook some of those mistakes and go on.

Numerous mistakes have been made in the alleged cause of Christ. I remind you that for all of the mistakes, there are 350,000 congregations in the United States that are meeting the spiritual needs of people. These same congregations have missionaries all over the world. They send them out. They support them. They make it happen. These missionaries often live and serve in conditions we would not tolerate for one minute. But, that is the extent of their dedication and their commitment to the cause of Christ. Those 350,000 congregations across America have thousands upon thousands of volunteers involved in jail ministry, food pantries, support groups and service organizations throughout the community.

Starting Over With Your Church

Peter Drucker, the notorious management consultant, said that entertainment is the largest export of the U.S.A. He quickly added to that statement, "The large church is the single most significant social movement in the world today." His insights included this exciting thought, "Our next big export will be voluntarism and charity." This is what the church of Jesus Christ is all about. In John it says, "It does not yet appear what we shall be." When you believe that, you can start over and overlook some of the abuses and some of the mistakes of the church.

If you are going to start over with the church, you have to get beyond the beginning. What do you mean by that? It is typified for me by the little fellow that was sound asleep, but fell out of his bed. Has that ever happened to you? Has it ever happened at your house? You know you hear that terrible bang, and you go in there, and the parent says, "What happened?" That is one of the dumbest questions you could ever ask. The poor little person is sprawled on the floor trying to figure it out and you say, "What happened?" One little guy said, "I went to sleep too near the place I got in."

In a sense, friends, that is a parable of many of the people in the kingdom of God. We go to sleep too near the place where we got in. Our first blush of enthusiasm, when the love of Christ has touched us and we feel a sense of forgiveness and peace and hope, somehow fades. We not only look pale. We are pale. We let that be not just the beginning of our Christian pilgrimage, we let it be the ending. There is no sense of discipleship. There is so sense of growth. But, that is only the beginning. There is no risk to that. Somebody said if it's true that our sins crucify the Lord afresh, then our mediocrity buries him again. Our mediocrity does not heal the love-ache that is at large in our world. Mediocrity will not make any impact. I do not believe any program in the church ought to be mediocre. I think we are about something that is of the very best of God. The promises of Scripture say we have power to become children of God. "To all who receive him, who believed in his name, he gave power to become children of God." John 1:12. God is not interested in a self-development program for us or in the enhancement of our self-esteem. God is interested in transformation, a complete redo of our sense of being and our purpose in life. Going to church no more makes you a Christian than running a wheel-barrow through a garage makes you an automobile. No way! You have to be in touch with the transforming power of the Holy Spirit.

When Peter Marshall, a Presbyterian pastor, was chaplain to the Senate of the United States, he made this insightful observation, "You cannot build a different world with indifferent people."

For many social organizations, you have to get your credentials up. Somebody has to endorse you. Somebody has to embellish what you have to offer to get you in. If you want to become a member of a country club or a golf club, three or four members have to put you up and affirm that you can pay the bills or that you will not cheat. Or, if you want to become a member of Rotary, somebody has to sponsor you. The same is true of the Lions club, the Exchange Club, the Kiwanis club, frater-nities and sororities. If you want to move up in the Cub Scout organization, you have to have somebody endorse you. Somebody has to write a letter of reference for you. If you want to join the Junior League, you had better have some sponsors.

The church is unique in our culture. It is the one society where you have to affirm that you are unworthy of membership. You have to affirm that, "Hey, I'm not much. I'm just a sinner and I need God's grace." But, you have to get beyond the beginning. Don't stop at the start. The beginning is far from the ending!

Someone asked Peter Drucker, an Episcopalian, "If you had one word to say to the churches, what would it be?" Without hesitation Drucker replied, "Give as much time as you can to the new and as little time as possible to that which is dying."

It is God's church. It is the spirit of God that makes it all happen. It is not your church. It is not my church. The word of God is preached. The word of God is taught. The word of God is acted out. A sense of the presence of God is felt. Manifestations of power are experienced. The love of God is revealed. The unity of God is perceived. Those are all items that help us meet the love-ache in people. So, if you are going to start over with the church and be serious about meeting the love-ache, you start with worship. You get serious about prayer. You get intentional about Bible study. You get deliberate about some form of service. You get motivated about witnessing to the evidence of the power of God at work in your life.

Lou Holtz of Notre Dame has been honored as college coach of the year. Wherever Holtz has coached, he has managed to put winners on the field and the right numbers on the scoreboard. Fascinating personality. In

1966, when he was thirty-nine years old, he sat down and wrote out his goals and dreams for life. He put them in various categories: professional, personal, and financial. He added categories like travel and exciting things to do. He ended up with these five categories. His list of goals and dreams totalled 107. Some of them he has already accomplished, like having dinner at the White House. Can you imagine Lou Holtz at the White House? He has accomplished that. He also wanted to own a 1949 Chevy. He has done that. But, he has some other goals he wants to accomplish. He wants to jump out of an airplane. He wants to cruise in a submarine. He wants to float down the Snake River some summer and experience the white water. His philosophy is don't be a spectator! Don't let life pass you by!

I extend the same invitation in terms of the church of Jesus Christ. Don't be a spectator. Don't let it pass you by. It is so easy to be on the outside looking in and criticize and recant the hypocrisy.

When our daughter Sheri finished the ninth grade, she looked forward to a summer of freedom. At fifteen, life was a series of fun adventures.

Since Linda would be traveling to a variety of music conferences, Sheri would be alone with time on her hands and no supervision throughout most of the summer.

I decided to help her fill the time. One of the suggestions I made was that she join the Grace Church youth group on a mission project prescribed by the Presbyterian church in the Yucatan Peninsula of Mexico. The idea brought the torrent of excuses and rejection. "I don't know anybody in the youth group." "I don't want to work in the jungle." "I am not going." "I will get sick drinking the water."

I exercised my option of parental power. I told her she was going. Fight it, she did. I insisted she raise the money and go. Reluctantly, she did.

Ten days later, I wish you could have been with me to greet her at the airport upon their arrival back in Houston. She was ecstatic. She loved it. She wouldn't stop talking about her new friends in the church, the hard work she did hauling cement, the intrigue of the Mayan people, the newly won respect for Christian missions, the beauty of the peninsula, and much more. This was a changed person. She also told me, and best of all, of her newfound faith in Jesus Christ.

I was thrilled. Everything I could have wished for her to experience—physically, emotionally and spiritually—had transpired. It was all I could do to see the road as I drove her home because of my tears of joy. Sheri had started over with the church.

You are welcome. You can enjoy the security of being part of the body of Christ. In the church, God promises fire. Not some faint, flickering flame, but real fire. That is the fire of Pentecost. The power of the Holy Spirit, gifts and all. Enough to make things happen beyond anything you might conceive. You are invited to dream holy dreams. You are also called to light. Not some dim bulb. You are called according to the Scriptures to be a city set on a hill. That is how bright you are supposed to be. You are supposed to emulate joy no matter where you are. No giddy happiness! You are called to emulate the joy of finding a radiant treasure, a solution to that love-ache in people's lives. To know the satisfaction of hungering and thirsting after God.

Do you remember the comedian Henny Youngman? He was famous for his one-liners. One time he was thrown out of an antiques shop. "All I did," he said, "was walk in and ask, 'What's new?' "

Today is an unspoiled new day. Question. Does the newness come from your calendar or your character? New Testament Greek differentiated between the two types of new. One word meant "point of time." The other word meant "point of nature." New Testament scholar William Barclay clarified it: "A newly manu-factured pencil is NEOS (new in point of time); but a man who was once a sinner and is now on the way to being a saint is KANIOS (new in point of nature)."

Today is your new day. Your opportunity to start over. Start over with the church and God will satisfy your love-ache.

CHAPTER THREE

Starting Over
With Your Dreams

Philippians 4:10-13

Christopher Nolan received the prestigious British Whitbread Award. Christopher was honored because he wrote a book entitled *Under The Eye Of The Clock.* The book is spectacular. It is autobiographical in nature. It is the story of Christopher's struggle for meaning in life. It deserves recognition. Why? Because Christopher was brain damaged when he was born. He can only communicate with his eyes.

In painstaking fashion, Christopher put this book together. He has a band he wears around his head. Out of his band extends a pen-like piece. He taps out the words. One page demands hours of deep concentration. The pace is agonizingly slow. But he did it. What was it that enabled this boy to realize his dream? His own verdict is, "I can't make my damned body do anything." His body imprisons this spectacular mind. How is he able to do it? He said, at age three, he recognized a spark in

27

his life. He knew that he was alive. He knew that he was loved. He knew that he was wanted. That was enough. It enabled him to pursue his dream.

What is poverty? Is it when somebody is broke? Is it when somebody is homeless? Is it when somebody is hungry? No, I really believe poverty is when someone has no dreams. Lacking dreams is a tragedy. I enjoy asking people the question, "What are you looking forward to?" I know the question leaves much to be desired grammatically, but it provokes an answer that gives me a clue as to how well the other person is dealing with life. If your dreams are dashed to the extent that you look forward to nothing, then you have a major concern. If you answer that question with some sparkle in the eye and some inflection of enthusiasm in the voice, it indicates some optimism concerning the future.

You need to look forward to something. If the future is bleak and holds no excitement of promise for you then you need to do some assessment of your life. "What are you looking forward to?" If the answer is "nothing" then it is time to get some help. If the answer is simple: "I am looking forward to seeing my family on vacation." "I am looking forward to riding my bicycle next Saturday." "I am looking forward to dinner with my friends at Chili's." "I am looking forward to reading that novel on the best-seller list." Looking forward does not have to be expensive or dangerous. It may be something as simple as taking a walk or catching a quick nap. But it indicates a future and an orientation. That is important. How are you doing? Are you leaning toward the future? Or are you just allowing the future to happen?

Starting Over With Your Dreams

Christians believe that God is above us, around us, within us, and also that God is ahead of us. Abraham Maslow looks at the future and says we approach it with either the "growth choice" or the "fear choice." I believe that God is the "growth choice" as opposed to the "fear choice"; that God cares about us in terms of the present; but that God also draws us into the future, encouraging us to take some risks, pushing us to dream and daring us to reach beyond our grasp. The Apostle Paul writes, "I can do all things through Christ," not in his own strength. "I can do all things through Christ who strengthens me." Again, Paul pushes us in II Corinthians 4:16, "We do not lose heart." Though our outer nature is wasting away, God renews our inner nature every day; that somehow God infuses mysteriously within us a sense of purpose, a goal, a redemptive participation, maybe even a dream to be realized for his glory.

Soak in this beautifully written prayer:

"O God, grant not that I be sheltered
from dangers, but fearless in facing them.
I pray not for the stilling of my pain, but
for a heart to bear it. Grant me the
blessing of success, but even more let me
find the grasp of your hand in the future."

When you walked the beach and watched the sun go down, you were given a spectacular display of beauty. The colors, the clouds and the changes all overwhelm you. You look out across the water and all you see is the horizon. What is the horizon? The horizon is really nothing more than the limit of our sight. Our sight is so limited. God has a plan beyond the horizon for us. God sees beyond the horizon. It is okay to dream. Real poverty is not having any dreams.

One day I had lunch with Frances Smith, a member of my congregation. She is in her eighties and an active ham radio operator. Her career as an educator spills over into many other areas of interests to this day. She is creative, alert, and always ready to pursue a raw idea. I told her, "I'm preaching on dreams this Sunday." I said, "At your stage of the game..." (I was trying to be very careful, respectful, and cautious), "do you still have any dreams? What do you dream about? Have you realized all your dreams? Do you still have some dreams?" And she said, "Oh yes, Dave." She did not even hesitate. I said, "Well, I am interested to know." This is what she said, "I'm dreaming of the day when we've got a space station up there and I can see it on television." Isn't that marvelous? You could have blown me away. I would have never guessed that was something she anticipated with enthusiasm. She has a sense of the future. She is future oriented!

Back in the Depression, in the early thirties, a panel of speakers addressed a black audience on the south side of Chicago. It was the south side of Chicago that Sinatra made famous in the song "Chicago". At that time, on the south side of Chicago, there was severe economic depression. Money and jobs were difficult if not impossible to find. There was very little by way of optimism. Nobody really had any dreams. They did not know where to look or where to go.

A panel of experts were drawn together to discuss the situation. Clarence Darrow was one of the panelists. Darrow, the distinguished attorney and professed atheist, took his turn addressing the crowd. He laid out their plight. He beautifully articulated their case. As he added up the woes, it appeared there was no hope. There was nothing there. Then, he stopped and he turned to that black audience and he said, "And yet you sing. No one can sing like you do. What do you have to sing about?"

In a flash, a woman out of the audience spoke up and said, "We can sing about Jesus." And with that, there was a torrent of vocal response out of that audience to Clarence Darrow. He was not prepared for what followed. Shouts blanketed the auditorium. It was "Amen!" and "Yes!" and "That's right!" They let it fly as only an African-American audience can do. This dumbfounded Darrow. It left him dazed and baffled as to the appropriate response, because he was face-to-face with the mysterious. The unexplainable confronted him, a hope that lives above our fears and tears. They had a sense that God held them somehow; that there was a hand there to clasp them and theirs in the midst of their failures. "I can do all things through Christ." Not through his own strength, Paul said, "but through Christ who strengthens me."

My wife and good friend, Linda, is a gifted keyboard artist. Her degree is in pipe organ. However, her first love has always been piano. For more than twenty-five years, she has been involved professionally in music. Countless times, she has mixed classical piano themes with familiar gospel hymns and presented them as an offering of thanksgiving to God in worship. She feels very deeply that her keyboard gift is a sacred trust that she is to use for the glory of God. For years, people have urged Linda to record some of her arrangements and publish them. She put it off until October of 1988. Then, she got serious. She rented a Los Angeles recording studio and laid down some of her piano tracks. She enhanced those items by accompanying herself on a synthesizer. The end result is a beautiful recording entitled "Classic Gospel." It's popularity has amazed Linda. But more than realizing one of her dreams, the impact of this musical ministry has astounded her. Notes, phone calls and conversations tell Linda of the joy her music has provided. Here are some samples: "Linda, your music is the only thing that quieted my mother's anxiety after her stroke while in the nursing home." "I don't know if it will have the same effect on most people, but while I was listening to Linda play, I missed my turn at Seguin and almost went to San Antonio."

"Thank you for your lovely recording. I do <u>not</u> share it. I keep it in <u>my</u> car, because once I put it in the player, my driving stress is washed away. 'Fairest Lord Jesus' has been my favorite since childhood."

"My driving habits have improved since receiving your tape. I slow down so that I do not arrive at my destination before the end of one of your songs."

"I listen to your tape in my car. It keeps me focused on God's grace even in the midst of a Houston traffic jam."

"Tears filled my eyes when I heard your music. A friend gave it to me for Christmas. It brought back pleasant memories of the wonderful relationship I had with my father and the hymns he loved to sing."

That recording was a substantial financial and emotional investment for us personally. But, the spiritual dividends have been beyond our wildest dreams. Linda has now made numerous recordings on the Brentwood label. We dared to dream that Linda should share her talent with others. Humankind has an amazing capacity to cope. People cope with all kinds of things. But for the Christian, for the one who has accepted Jesus Christ as Savior, for that person, there is an added dimension of strength because God promises you the dynamic power of the Holy Spirit. God promises you gifts of the Spirit of God to empower you to deal honestly and creatively with whatever the future brings. In addition to that, you have added another dimension, the support of the Christian community.

I am uncomfortable holding it up to be paraded, highlighted or spotlighted. But it happens at Grace Presbyterian Church, Houston, day after day after day. Because of that dimension of power of the Holy Spirit and the dramatic support of the Christian community, people dare to dream.

At Grace Church, the Discovery Class consists mainly of young couples. They are educated, aggressive achievers. They are the kind of people that can choose to make a difference in this world.

Our Presbytery's refugee resettlement program hit me with a challenge. Our church had helped settle Vietnamese refugees in the past, so why not another challenge? This opportunity for growth came in the form of a Cambodian refugee family. It involved money, time, and some hands-on action. I took the story to the Commitment Committee of our Session and the Discovery Class. Both responded graciously. Their commitment and enthusiasm began to build. The Vanly

Ouk family became important to this segment of our membership. Vanly, his wife, and five children came to Houston, found other family members, got jobs, food, housing, furnishings, transportation and medical care. They are contributing citizens to this community. Their joy is contagious. Why did it happen? Because a group of Christians opted for the "growth choice" rather than the "fear choice."

Ralph Waldo Emerson said, "What lies behind us and what lies before are small matters compared to what lies within us." The Scripture says, "Christ in you the hope of glory."

A pastor was walking down the street in Hong Kong. He walked past a tattoo shop. Displayed in the window of the tattoo shop were designs you could have tattooed on your body. There were anchors, there was "Mother," there were snakes, there were crosses, there were flags. Then, there was this phrase, "Born to Lose." The pastor could not take it. He stopped and went into the shop and talked to the Chinese tattoo artist. The owner was asked, "Seriously, does anyone really have that phrase 'Born to Lose' tattooed on their body?" The little Chinese man said, "Yes, sometimes." The pastor replied, "I can't believe it. How could anybody in their right mind have that sort of statement 'Born to Lose' tattooed on their body?" The little Chinese man tapped his forehead and said in broken English, "Before tattoo on body, tattoo on mind." What do you have tattooed on your mind? Is it fear, failure, freedom, fortune or faith. God wants tattooed on your mind "Child of God."

How do you start over with your dreams? Two suggestions. One is, dare to dream. You can dare to dream. We go through life trying to make everybody happy, trying to please everybody. We are conditioned to conform. Oliver Wendell Holmes said, "Most of us die with the music still in us." I do not believe that is God's will for you. For you to die with the music still in you is to miss out on God's good intentions for the use of your gifts. You do not have to die with the music still in you.

Recently, Henry Moore died. Henry Moore, along with Rodin and Michelangelo, belongs to a very small group, a handful of great sculptors in this world. Henry Moore was born in Yorkshire, England. His father worked in the mines. He was the seventh child in that family. He knew very little of affluence, education, or prestige. His background was, at best, modest. He enjoyed going to Sunday school. That was where his dreams began. When he was ten years old, he realized he could draw. He also understood that he had unique abilities as a whittler. He enjoyed doing things with his hands. He liked his Sunday school teacher. He had never heard anything like the stories his teacher told before. The Sunday school teacher talked about Michelangelo. He referred to Michelangelo as the greatest sculptor in all of history. A light went on in Henry's mind. He contemplated, "Maybe I can be a great sculptor. Maybe I could be the greatest sculptor of my day." Through imagination, super-abundant energy and real character, he dared to dream of greatness. He lifted himself up and made something of himself, and of course, became one of the great sculptors in the world. Why? Because he dared to dream.

Whenever the Super Bowl is played, I am part of that great audience of millions of viewers. We watch some coaches, owners, players, and fans pursue their dreams. They dare to dream. Some of those players dared to dream that they might be in a Super Bowl, not just for the check, not just for the ring, but for the experience of it. It represents success; a significant athletic achievement. They dared to dream they might be there. Of course, the Super Bowl is the most wagered sporting event anywhere at any time. People can bet on the point spread. People can bet on the winner. People can bet on the combined score. People can bet on who is going to score in the last two minutes of the first half. Somebody, said, "We make our money the old-fashioned way. We gamble for it." All the gamblers dream of monetary success. But, the Super Bowl game itself without all the hype does spotlight some young athletes that have dared to dream.

There is always somebody moving so fast in our age that they are ahead of us. Just as soon as we say, "Oh, it can't be done. It won't work out. It'll never happen," we are interrupted by the news that somebody's made it happen. Somebody's done it. There is no joy that grows out of the soil of cynicism. If you aim at nothing, you will hit it. As God's people, he calls us to dream holy dreams. I dare you to dream some holy dreams. Maybe it pertains to your relationships. Maybe it pertains to your vocation. Maybe it pertains to your resources. Maybe it pertains to your education. But, I dare you to dream some holy dreams. God has invested enormous power in you. How do you intend to actualize that potential?

I am convinced that if Western Christians could experience firsthand Christian missionary work in the

Third World, this would generate enough money to triple the investment. Why? Because of the credibility of Christian mission causes and the high caliber missionaries that make it happen. I believe Christians would thrill to the opportunity of sharing in that kind of redemptive enterprise. In addition to that, missionaries tend to get more "bang for the buck" than any other workers in government or non-profit organizations.

I have always been an advocate for mission trips. Each year, Grace Church sends youths and adults into remote areas of the world in response to requests for help, often hard labor, from missionaries. One of our pet projects is the Yucatan Peninsula of Mexico. There, clinics, orphanages, camps, and churches have benefitted from our investment. The beautiful payback is this: Grace Church has a stronger sense of community, a better informed membership concerning mission, and a personalized commitment to the enhancement of the Kingdom of God.

This type of experience took on a new dimension for Dr. James Kennedy, a maxillofacial surgeon. Jim and his wife, Sherry, felt the tug of the Holy Spirit to experience medical missions firsthand. Jim, a solo practitioner, decided to give up his practice for a month and devote that period of time to the Good Shepherd Presbyterian Hospital in Kananga, Zaire. It was no small sacrifice for a popular person like Jim to give up his successful practice for a full month and pay his staff salaries for that period of time. Just because Jim took off does not mean he could forget his overhead. At his own expense, he traveled to and from Zaire, covering all of his costs. Jim came back a changed man. He now is an effective catalyst for medical missions. Whenever he tells his story of Zaire and shows his slides, his experience moves people to greater Christian commitment. It became a dream realized for Sherry and Jim.

Dr. Kennedy sent this letter to me shortly after his arrival in Zaire. It gives a hint as to the impact that experience had on his life.

February 7, 1989

Dear Dave,

I arrived in Africa to a different reception than I had anticipated. I was hassled by the airport custom officials and the Chief Inspector had all my baggage opened and examined. They thought that the footlocker with mail to the missionaries had money in it and I had to explain that it was only mail. Well, after 2½ hours, I finally cleared customs to enter a slum of 3 million people.

I have never seen filth, garbage, and poverty so great in my 48½ years. They (Zairians) don't have back door or front yard garbage pick-up. They just leave it in the streets, sidewalks, around buildings and everywhere you look, there is garbage. The poor people (the majority of the residents) pick thru for food and something to sell or use. The smell is everywhere and you have to fight back the nausea that surrounds you.

Today, I visited the University of Kinshasa Dental School where I was *introduced to the Dean. He is an oral & maxillofacial surgeon trained in Brussels. He asked me to consult on a child 3 years of age with a <u>Giant</u> Cystic Hygroma which protrudes from the tongue and mouth and will obstruct the airway in a few months. The doctors here at the school have never treated a case like this. I am sure this poor child will die before I leave Africa. These people of Africa have a very great <u>need</u>!*

The missionaries that I am living with are great people. They exemplify the life of Christ. I feel inferior and weak when I realize the sacrifices these missionaries have made.

I leave for Kananga Wednesday morning early and I am eager to get to work. I miss my family very much and I miss my family at Grace very much, also. God is teaching me patience, but it's a hard lesson.

I guess the Lord is softening my heart and opening my eyes to his grace. Dave, we at Grace are blessed more than we can ever realize. I just wish each member of our congregation could see what I have seen in just a few days. I am sure it would change their lives and open their hearts to the real meaning of stewardship. I thank you for being my minister and teaching me how to grow in my faith. I even miss hearing <u>your sermons</u>.

Your friend,
Jim

Let's Start Over

In spite of the sacrifice made by Jim and Sherry, they successfully concluded their fiscal year. He said, "God's blessing is real. It was our best year ever financially, even including the month out of the practice in Zaire."

The second thing I say to you is this: if you are going to start over with your dreams, you have to be determined to see your dreams through to completion. That determination does not come easy. The other day, I opened a new bottle of ketchup. I do not know how they do it. They pack that substance in there so tight that it is almost impossible to get it out of the bottle. Do you ever get frustrated doing that? And then when the ketchup finally breaks free, it goes all over and just covers your hamburger, the plate, the pickle and everything surrounding it. You have a mess on your hands. I love that dear frustrated mother. She had all the hamburgers laid out at suppertime. The kids seated themselves at the counter waiting for supper. They were all set to go. She was trying to coax that ketchup out of that bottle. The phone rang and she said to her daughter, "Answer the phone and tell them I'll call them back later." So the child answered the phone and said, "My mother can't come to the phone now, she's hitting the bottle."

Alan Page is a member of the Pro Football Hall of Fame. He is now a Federal Judge. As an eleven year veteran of the Minnesota Vikings, Page often broke in new coaches. A new defensive line coach asked Page and some of his defensive linemen to read from a playbook. He sensed a foreign emotion to the 1978 Vikings, fear! Soon after the coach passed out the playbooks, it was obvious that four of his nine teammates on the defensive line did not know how to read.

I will never forget the television clip of Dexter Manley, the free-spirited, sometimes outrageous Washington Redskins defensive end before a Senate panel.

He said, "It was very difficult because I felt I was normal, but I was told I was dumb and stupid. Athletics was the only thing that built some self-esteem, some self-worth."

At times during his presentation before the Senate panel, Manley began to stumble. Sweat rolled down his cheeks and tears of frustration filled his eyes. There were long pauses. He spoke of receiving nineteen grades of "F" in second grade and being placed in a special education class for four years. He was pushed through high school and played football for Oklahoma State University despite a severe learning disability that effectively rendered him illiterate.

Manley, at age thirty, enrolled in classes at Washington's LAB School. They judged him to have a second-grade reading level when he entered.

"I had to humble myself," he said. "I had to walk into the LAB School and not pretend. Today, I can read and write. I have some self-respect."

There are twenty-seven million functionally illiterate adults in the United States. These people cannot read a pharmacist's prescription, a child's report card, or a warning label on a pesticide container.

Dexter Manley had a dream and the determination to realize it through to fruition. For him to learn to read took more courage than anything he had ever done on the football field.

Let's Start Over

It does take determination to see our dreams through to fruition. Any dead fish can float downstream. H.L. Mencken wrote: "A cynic is a man who, when he smells flowers, looks around for a coffin." It takes a determined live fish to swim upstream against the current in life. You are a privileged people. God calls you to dream. God plants some holy dreams in your psyche. Individually and corporately, you are part of the body of Christ. You are unique. I remind you that your faith in God is "either a dull habit or it is an acute fever."

We talk all the time about "Ah, so-and-so's a lost cause. He's a lost cause. She's a lost cause. That's a lost cause. It'll never work." There is no lost cause in God's redemptive program. The cross of Jesus Christ is elevated for all the world to see. We must have looked like a lost cause to God and God sent his son, and the Scripture says, "not to condemn the world, but that the world through him might be saved." There really are no great people in the world. Are you aware of that? There really are no great people in this world. There are ordinary people trying to do extraordinary things. Trying to see holy dreams through to completion. It takes determination. It implies commitment.

George Smith was a Christian missionary to Africa for the Moravian church. He was only there a couple of months when he was forced to leave. This particular country in Africa decided to shut down missionary work, expel all of the foreigners, and George Smith was gone. He left, but he left in depression, frustrated because he really had only one woman make a profession of faith in Christ.

He went home leaving this one convert behind. One old woman. When George got home, he really was discouraged because of all the money that had been invested in him, all the time that had been spent, all the preparations that had been made so that he could give his life to missionary work in Africa, and the conclusion was frustration. In fact, he soon died. He died on his knees praying for the people that he loved in Africa. One hundred years later, that ministry to the old woman blossomed.

The seeds of truth George planted grew to fruition. What a harvest! A hundred years later, they discovered in that particular area thirteen thousand happy Christians.

Ephesians 3:20, says God "is able to do far more abundantly than all that we ask or think..." In high school, I was told to get out, that I was a bum, that I was simply taking up space at Glebe Collegiate Institute. I really was viewed as a waste. There was not a lot of hope for me. I had disappointed others. I, too, was disappointed. A young minister came along and said, "Dave, you're wasting your life. Why don't you turn it over to God? I believe God's got something good for you, something better in mind than what you're doing!"

He invited me to work at his camp in sports and in music. At the camp, each night we would pray. He was smart enough to keep me in his cabin. But when we would get in, he would have prayer, and it was not a "sweat you" prayer. No high pressure. It was not a prayer of condemnation. It was very conversational prayer. Often, he would not just pray at me, he would pray for me with genuine compassion. One night after he

43

prayed, he stopped and he said, "Dave, wouldn't you like to commit your life to Christ? I really believe God has something for you." And I did. I was sincere. I was serious.

In that same week, I remember catching in a softball game. I was the catcher for both teams. Nobody in their right mind serves as catcher for both teams. But I was the combination catcher for both teams, cheerleader, and umpire. That way I could at least be fair. Bad calls for both teams! I clearly remember catching and thinking, "You know, I don't have to end up working in business. I don't have to sell insurance. I don't have to be a lawyer. I don't have to be a banker. I don't have to be a CPA. Maybe I could spend my life doing something in terms of ministry for God's glory. Maybe I could help people in the same way that young pastor helped me."

I never dreamed that I would end up in the ministry. I never dreamed that I would have the privilege of pastoring a great, dynamic congregation like Grace Presbyterian, Houston. The only words I know to express it are really from George Herbert, "Who would have thought my shriveled heart could have recovered greenness." I dared to dream. Then I was determined to see that dream through to completion. Thank God, the Divine source is not done with me yet.

I dare you to dream some holy dreams. What would it be in terms of your life? What dreams do you have for the enhancement of the Kingdom of God? The tougher question follows: What do you intend to do to see them through to completion? Can you make the sacrifice? I can attest from my experience. It is worth it.

Starting Over With Your Dreams

When Rudyard Kipling was trying to get published, he was told, "You just don't know how to use the English language."

George Orwell's most famous book is *Animal Farm.* When he tried to find a publisher in the United States, he was informed, "Animal stories don't sell in the U.S.A."

Walt Disney was fired by his first editor because he had, "No creative ideas."

Charles Schultz of *Peanuts* fame could not get his cartoons published in his high school yearbook.

Michael Jordon, the former National Basketball Association superstar, was cut from the squad when he first tried out for his high school basketball team.

I dare you to pray that God will not only implant some fresh dreams in you, but also that these dreams will happen by the Spirit of God. Karl Barth, the twentieth century's leading Reformed Theologian said, "To clasp hands in prayer is the beginning of an uprising against the disorder of the world."

Pray to that end. Your dreams will give you a new start in life.

CHAPTER FOUR

Starting Over With Your Family

Ephesians 6:1-4

A teenage babysitter had a tough job. She was assigned to two young children. It was a horrible night because these two children fought with each other throughout the evening. She had to fight with them to get them to go to bed. She had little success. She even tried to bribe them. She gave them cookies and milk. They proceeded to spill the milk and cookies and then stomp the mess into the carpet. Finally, she got them to go to bed. But, she could not get them to stay in bed. It was a devastating experience for her. The parents had promised to be in at midnight. They arrived at 2 a.m. She greeted them at the door as she heard the key go in the lock. She said, "Oh, don't apologize. I wouldn't be in a hurry to come home to them either."

Relationships make this world go round. When Robert Bartley was the editor of the *Wall Street Journal,* he addressed a graduating class and gave them this insight, "The most serious ethical problem you will face will not be a business problem, but a family problem. Managing your obligations to your spouses, to your children, and to your aging parents." No human experience influences human nature more than the family experience. It is of that much importance.

We all have a neurotic need for material security. We work very hard at that. We drive ourselves. It is a compulsion for us. But in truth, what we really need is emotional security. No matter how much material security we have, it has little to do with emotional security.

The Harris Poll people asked, "What is the most important thing in life?"

Despite all the flotsam and jetsam of the born-to-shop generation, 96% said "What we want above everything else is to have a strong family life."

There is a magnetism to family commitments.

The family is no accident. It is part of the Divine design.

Jesus knew how important relationships would be to us and so he summed up the commandments, "O Jerusalem, Jerusalem, killing the prophets and stoning those who are sent to you! How often would I have gathered your children together as a hen gathers her brood under her wings, and you would not! Behold, your house is forsaken and desolate. For I tell you, and you will not see me again, until you say, 'Blessed is he who comes in the name of the Lord.' " (Matthew 23:37-40) In essence, Jesus really gave us a summary of the commandments. He admonished, "You shall love the Lord your God with all your heart, and with all your soul, and with all your

47

mind." To that great and first commandment he added, "You shall love your neighbor as yourself."

Relationships make us or break us. Our lives revolve around relationships. They are extremely important to us. How do they happen? By thought, by proximity, by time, by accessibility, by community, by sacrifice, and by effort. The Apostle Paul knows that! He writes in Ephesians 6 about the investment that is required to make relationships work. Under the umbrella of God's love in Jesus Christ, you are supposed to step out of yourself, take a look at the needs that are around you, assess them, and then get serious about doing something about them. He directs his comments to children and to parents, to slaves and the masters, to employers and employees, and to people like you and me. Paul knows our tendency to cave in to peer pressure. He begs us not to be crowd pleasers! You gain nothing in that. God calls us to be servants of Jesus Christ. If you serve Jesus Christ, that requires thought, time, effort, accessibility, and sacrifice. To fully comprehend that is the key that unlocks this passage. To appreciate Ephesians 6, you must go back a few lines to Ephesians 5, verse 21. "Be subject to one another out of reverence for Christ." That subjection is not subservience. It is a choice. It is not a chance. It is not throwing caution to the wind. It is a choice you make on the basis that you can trust, experience, and emulate the love of Jesus Christ.

In the late 1940's, C.C. Zimmerman, a sociologist predicted that, "We are directly bound to reach the conclusion that unless some unforeseen Renaissance occurs the family system will continue headlong its present trend toward nihilism."

Starting Over With Your Family

It sure sounds like he was saying "Get ready to bury the family!"

Zimmerman speaks for many social scientists who believe that family life as we have known it is on track for destruction. Nihilism is not too strong a word. Is the family a rapidly dying institution? Before we bury the family, there are some other factors that are worthy of a closer look.

It is true that the number of divorces and unmarried couples living together continue to increase. Our pattern of life separates families. Our life-style demands a broader economic base. That places economic, physical, and emotional demands on families. Day care, after school programs, lessons, and leagues all play a role in the shaping of our life-style.

Is the family an anachronism, hopefully out of synchronization with this age?

There is a magnetism to family life. Divorced people, though badly hurt and scarred through a previous marriage, are willing to marry again.

Mary Jo Bane in the title of her book declares *The American Family Is Here To Stay.* She wrote, "The facts...about marriage, child rearing, and family ties in the United States today provide convincing evidence that family commitments are likely to persist in our society. Family ties, it seems clear, are not archaic remnants of a disappearing traditionalism, but persistent manifestations of human needs for stability, continuity, and nonconditional affection."

In a world in which people feel more and more depersonalized, the family is a necessary ingredient for meeting needs of intimacy.

Let's Start Over

From the very first pages of the Old Testament, marriage and family leap out as part of God's created order. Marriage and family is not an afterthought of God. It is the only human institution antedating the "fall" of humankind. God is the prototype of the parental pattern. God's relationship to us as the children of God is a pattern for all social relationships. God is parent not just in name, but also in nature.

Christian families ought to be different. I believe that Christian families should be different from the rest of the world. Christianity ought to make our families freer. Freer from resentment, tension, stress, and strife. Freer than non-Christian families. Why? Because we live under the shadow of the cross. The mercy, the forgiveness, the grace of God in Jesus Christ, ought to have made a difference in our relationships. Some genius wrote, "You can pick your friends, but you only can inherit your family." Lots of us would like to redo that deal and pick our family, and instead inherit some friends. William James Durant, the man who did such an enormous study on the history of civilization concluded, "The family is the nucleus of civilization." That is not from a religious writer. That is not out of the Bible. That is a secular human being looking at this planet and saying, "The family is the nucleus of civilization."

The one factor that influences character development and emotional security for an individual is the relationship that person had with both parents as a child. It is that significant. To a child, the absence or the inaccessibility of a parent, be it physical or emotional, as a result of divorce or death or a time demanding job has a profound effect on the mental health of a child. What is the greatest fear that an infant has? It is abandonment. "Don't leave me alone." When a family begins to disintegrate, we know the cost because feelings so often focus on loss, a sense of abandonment. Do professional relationships help? Yes, they do. But they never, never can provide the kind of emotional sustenance that a caring, sensitive, warm family relationship can provide. We know that if an individual is in trouble, the whole family is in trouble. They are not unconnected or disconnected. That is why Jesus talked so much about relationships. He knew what made us tick. He knew what our real deep emotional needs were all about. So relationships are our priority.

On numerous occasions, Linda and I have been asked, "How have you been able to sustain such a good relationship with your children?"

One of the reasons that we have had a positive experience with our children is honesty. We have been very honest with our children about such things as money, power, relationships, feelings, and goals. We have not attempted to disguise our feelings. We have been candid about such delicate items as human sexuality and our financial resources.

Our children know that they can raise any issue, ask any question and discuss any topic without embarrassment to us. They know that they will receive an honest response. We love our children enough to be honest with them. We want them to be able to count on our candor and counsel throughout life.

There is a sign in a nursery. Not the kind that has diapers, but the kind of nursery where you have fertilizers, sprays, grass seed, plants, flowers, and gardening tools. In that nursery, there is a big sign that shouts, "The time to plant a tree was 25 years ago." Thanks a lot! Big help!

I have enjoyed asking people, wherever I go, a sure conversation instigator. "If you could live your life over, what would you do differently?" Everyone has an opinion on that one. The answer I get back over and over again is, "Dave, I'd do something different about my family."

How do you start over with your family? Do I have any credentials to address this? I think so. Linda and I have been married better than twenty-nine years. We have two children. I have never been surrounded by so much wisdom. I have never been so ignorant as when I am in a conversation with my children, Sheri and Peter. So, what I write comes out of my own heart and out of my own experience. Starting over. What would I do if I were starting over with my family?

The first thing I would do if starting over with my family is to express my love more openly. I would be freer in terms of expressing my love. Not just in terms of words, but reading the tone of voice and even the non-verbal communication. I would be more open, more honest about my successes, and also about my failures. I continue to make a very common mistake. The mistake I make is to assume everybody in the family knows that I love them. Surely they know how much I care about them. What could be more important than my love for God and family? I take them for granted. When that happens, they begin to take me for granted. With that, a kind of dullness, a kind of numbness sets in. The passion begins to get a little musty. The edge of concern dulls. My family needs to hear from me how much they mean to me. I need to have the courage to speak up and express my love.

True love is a visible, tangible, concrete thing. True love is something real, something touchable, something observable. Try expressing your love when it is least expected. Do something new and kind just for the fun of it!

Vivian is a woman in my congregation who has driven her Buick station wagon through the end of her garage on numerous occasions. Life is full of little kindnesses and little surprises. That is part of love. Surprising somebody with an expression of love is a wonderful interruption. One day, her husband Neal said to her, "Darling, come out to the garage and sit in your Buick. I want you to see something." He had strung from the rafters of the garage a string and tied to it a tennis ball. Now he said, "It's a very simple process. All you need to know is that when the tennis ball hits your windshield, stop!" Now that's a beautiful way to say "I love you." It is also a much better way to handle your anger than arguing, shouting, or losing your sense of emotional balance.

Say, when was the last time you surprised somebody and gave them a gift not for a birthday or whatever, just because you love them? When was the last time you did that? Or when was the last time you did a chore for somebody for no other reason than love? "Hey, you go sit down and read the newspaper. I'll clean up this kitchen." "I'll clean out the garage for you." "Let me help you. I would like to do that. It will make the chore easier."

Let's Start Over

Our son Peter was a student at Texas Christian University in Fort Worth. He was a "Radio, Television and Film" major. In spite of his disdain for mathematics and science courses, they were required.

One evening, he called with a sad story as to the extreme degree of difficulty he found in taking Introduction to Geology. He whined and complained. He wanted to get out of it. I felt he had not given it an honest shot. I told him so. He chose not to make the effort to pass that course. At 6 a.m. the next morning, I got out of bed and wrote Peter a note. I was angry. I was hot. I was disgusted. The words almost scorched the page. They were flammable! By 9 a.m., then seated at my desk in the office, I began to feel bad about the strong language I had used on Peter denigrating his effort. It was too late to retrieve the letter. I had already mailed it. Peter had only experienced my tough side.

As I sat there wallowing in my guilt over my lack of sensitivity, I searched my mind for a means to let Peter see my tender side. Scanning the therapeutic ideas on my mind, I settled on a course of action. I called a friend Betty Ann at the Fredlyn Nut Company and asked her to send a pound of pistachios to Peter and bill me. I knew how much he loved pistachios. This was my way of attempting to balance toughness and tenderness.

Oh yes! Peter managed a "C" in Introduction to Geology.

I am inclined to show only my tough side. Maybe it is because my tender side is so tender. I use the toughness as a protector for the tenderness I feel. Good relationships strike a balance between toughness and tenderness.

Starting Over With Your Family

A member of my congregation sends me terrible cards from time to time...horrible things! But, it is refreshing in the midst of a hectic day to get something strange and humorous. It is a little levity. I need that. We all need that. If parents can model a loving relationship for their children, it gives them a kind of emotional security that they so desperately seek. If I were starting over with my family, I would show my love more openly.

The second thing I would do if starting over with my family is laugh more. That is right! I would laugh more. Not laugh at 'em, but laugh with 'em. "Humor is the hand of God on the shoulder of a weary world." Kids are forever coming up with these riddles or those corny little jokes. Sometimes, they have created a little stunt or a little trick. There is nothing wrong with just relaxing and enjoying the moment. We so often live for the future, we seldom give the moment any time.

We have a dumb thing at our house that happens whenever we have dinner in the dining room. Sheri started it! Somebody takes the challenge of trying to light all the candles in the dining room with one match. Big deal! But for some reason, that little challenge has caught on. When someone successfully lights them all with one match, that person gets to extinguish the match by dunking it in someone's drink. We have learned to laugh at that and not fight over it.

During my sermons, when Sheri sits in the congregation, she rates my humor. That is right. She rates them on a scale of one to five. Nobody else in the congregation knows this is going on. Just occasionally, I'll say something and suddenly see three fingers pop up from Sheri. If you don't think that breaks the momentum of the sermon, you're wrong! I smile. I need that. It also proves she is listening.

I smiled when Brad told me his wife had discovered a book entitled, *Potty Training In One Day.* He said, "It took her six months to read it, but in the meantime, the kid taught himself."

I need to laugh more at myself. I need to quit taking myself so seriously. When we take ourselves very seriously, that is when we are vulnerable to being easily hurt. If we can admit our faux pas, our mistakes, our sins, our errors, those around us can love us a little bit more. They may see us as truly human. Real people who hurt, who care, need a reciprocal relationship involving love. If I could start over with my family, I would laugh more.

The third thing I would do in starting over with my family is to listen more. That is tough to do because we are verbal people. I use my verbal skills to make a living. It is tough to tune in. Oh, it is easy to hear the verbiage. But, what I often miss, is the tone of voice which communicates so much more.

People who take dog-sledding seriously can tell by the bark of the dogs how well they are doing, how they are feeling, which dog is complaining, which dog is really hurting, and which dog is faking it. Now, if somebody can do that with animals, how much more should we as human beings be able to read the tone of voice. We ought to listen more. We all are busy. We all have demands placed on us. We all have high expectations for ourselves and others. But, God calls us to listen. Certainly, within the family relationship, we have an obligation to listen.

Have you read that the average fifteen year-old has asked 500,000 questions? Do you realize what a privilege that is as a parent? A half million opportunities to communicate something of your meaning in life, your philosophy of life, how you feel about life. What a privilege! When we really listen, that is an important expression of affirmation. To listen is really commendation. To refuse to listen is emotional deprivation. It is to hold back those things that might be damaging. Emotional deprivation is dangerous stuff. But, do not hold back those hugs, those pats, those apologies or those precious words "I love you" or "I forgive you."

Two men were standing on a soccer field watching their children play in a league game. One was the father of a young child. The child was off playing while the game was going on but he kept calling, "Hey Daddy, Daddy. Look over here, Daddy." The father ignored him. The friend that was standing with the father finally became conscious that the father was ignoring his child. Then, the father sensed that the friend had caught on that he was ignoring the child. So the father turned to the friend and said, "Aw, it's only the kid calling."

"It's only the kid calling." There will come a day when that child will become an adolescent and will say, "Aw, it's only the old man calling."

Brent Wilson has done some fascinating research focusing on the effect of family communication problems as a result of adolescent alcohol problems. His conclusion boiled down to this. "The more parents talked to and listened to their child, the more immune the child was to the persuasive influence of their peers to participate in heavy alcohol consumption."

Why is that? When parents show they care, no matter how awkward the expression of that care, it is a standard that is indelibly etched in the mind of the child. No one wants to demean a relationship of real trust. Caring parents give children guidelines for decision-making. Students without this family experience tend to have no opinions about alcohol or drugs and, when given the opportunity for abuse, are more easily persuaded to participate.

You should never underestimate peer pressure. In 1988, the Children's Defense Fund looked at data on teen sex practices and attitudes collected over ten years and issued a report. "Love is one of the least-named reasons teenagers give for having sex." The leading reason—peer pressure. "Everyone is doing it" does have an influence.

The fourth thing I would do if starting over with my family is to pray more. Yes, I am paid to pray. I am a pastor. In a sense, I am under contract to pray. Yes, I would pray more, I would pray differently. I would stop giving God directives. I would pray more for guidance. I would model prayer differently for them. I would set a standard for them. I would pray, not so much at them as pray for them. In the early morning hours when I wake up, I pray for my family, my staff, my congregation, and myself. I pray like this, "O Lord, make me fit to live with." I do not pray the nice verbiage that you get in a worship setting. This is the real stuff! When I say, "Lord make me fit to live with. Make me the kind of spouse, the kind of father, the kind of pastor, the kind of leader, the kind of boss, the kind of example that you would have me to be." I am really reaching for the counsel of the Holy Spirit. I put my feelings out there on the raw edge. I would pray more for guidance and that I might listen more attentively to the spirit of God speaking to me and even through me. If I were starting over with my family, I would pray more.

Fifth. If I were starting over with my family, I would handle my time differently. All of us have 168 hours before us each week. That is a huge block of time! Let's assume that everybody sleeps eight hours every night. So 56 hours of the 168 hours are designated for sleep. If we eat three meals per day over the next seven days that is 21 meals. Estimate roughly 30 minutes per meal. That may be too little or too much, so allow some flexibility and guess twelve hours for eating. Take twelve hours out of the 168 hours for eating. With busy metropolitan business people, it is safe to assume 60 hours for work per week with some travel time thrown in there. That still leaves us with 40 hours. What do we do with that 40-hour period every week?

Fortune magazine came out with a cover story entitled, "Why Grade 'A' Execs Get An 'F' As Parents." The corporate executive may be able to solve a substantial financial crisis in his or her organization with a few crisp commands. But, let that parent ask a teenage son why he got in late last night and he or she is reduced to impotent fury in seconds. "For all their brains and competence, powerful, successful executives and professionals often have more trouble raising kids than all but the very poor." Could it be that the intensity and single-mindedness that make for corporate achievement are often the opposite of the qualities you need for effective parenting?

Let's Start Over

Children cause us more stress and worry than anything else, including our careers. It is tough for kids growing up in families where the parents are highly successful. Raising happy, successful children is not a hopeless task or just dumb luck. The most important thing you can do for your child is to encourage a high sense of self-esteem. Easier said than done. True. The tricky part is helping children set appropriate, satisfying goals and then providing an environment that enables them to reach the goals on their own.

Just in case your long-range plans include working triple time at the office until your children turn seventeen, then deftly steering them into the Ivy League, this is for you. "Serious emotional problems usually start when children are in sixth to eighth grade, and hit crisis proportions by the sophomore year of high school." So says Sheila Ribordy, a clinical psychologist at De Pauw University.

All of us highly motivated types succeed with attributes such as perfectionism, impatience, and efficiency. These traits contrast directly with what it takes to meet the needs of a growing child—tolerance, patience, and acceptance of chaos. Given seventy hour work weeks, divorce, or a spouse with a career or a demanding social schedule, and complications set in fast.

How do you help them with their self-esteem? The top priority for parents is to help their children find something that makes them feel good about themselves. That is the greatest deterrent to drugs and alcohol. It does no good to greet your children every evening with an ostensibly cheery "How'd you do in school today?"

Starting Over With Your Family

That is a very threatening question. It often elicits no more than a mumbled "Okay."

You do not have to entertain every evening. Spend some time with your family. Book quality time into your schedule. Take that coaching responsibility. You can always put things off for the future. Unfortunately, you cannot get back the years with your children.

Instead of screaming at them, "You came home three hours late last night. Where were you?" How about trying, "When you don't call or come home at the time we have agreed on, I worry that something might have happened to you because I don't know where you are?"

I suppose the best insight I have received is that I should treat my children with the courtesy and sensitivity I reserve for my church officers, staff, and members of my congregation. By doing that, I believe my children will turn out to be some of my very closest friends. Remember, parents are very important to kids—much more so than they will ever let on.

Three hundred seventh and eighth graders were given the assignment of meticulously recording the time they spent with their parents. It was good research. They did the best that they could. But, the alarming statistic that came out of that was that the average amount of time that the father spent with a seventh or eighth grader in one week was seven and a half minutes. Do you think you are going to make any impact on kids if you are giving them seven and a half minutes out of a week? You can talk about all the social problems, but this is the basic problem, the amount of time and the quality of the time that we give to our kids. When you agree to give time to a child, be it a young child or even a teenager,

61

make it their time. Be there. And be there not just physically, but also emotionally. Tune in. It is amazing what you can learn.

Free time for Peter Lynch evaporated as the Magellan Fund grew. When he was forty-six years old and worth twenty million dollars, Peter Lynch decided it was time to retire. After thirteen years at the helm of the Magellan Fund, the man many consider the greatest portfolio manager of all time has called it quits. "I just want to spend more time with my family."

Lynch's decision to quit involved two competing worlds. The constant battle between family and career.

One of Lynch's colleagues said in awe, "It's unusual to just leave. But from his point of view, how loud can the applause get?" He is going out a winner. His purpose, to spend more time with his family. He discovered that even on Sunday mornings, he was working four hours prior to attending church. His father died at age 46, when Lynch was just 10 years old. He said, "you feel immortal when you still have parents alive. It sort of hits you when all of a sudden you're it."

A little guy was out in the backyard playing catch with his dad. They were throwing a football. He was enjoying the experience. They were having a good time. Suddenly the telephone rang and the mother came out to the backyard and called the husband in to the telephone. As the father went in the door to answer the phone, and the little guy was left tossing the football to himself, he turned to his mother and he said, "Don't you know that when Dad's with me he's busy!" There is a lot of truth to that. "When Dad's with me he's busy!"

Starting Over With Your Family

When you give your time to your child, it is really an emergency. It ought to be treated as an emergency. I don't know about you, but I can only handle one emergency at a time. How we prioritize our time indicates what relationships really matter to us.

Don't forget bedtime. Many children fear bedtime because it represents physical and emotional separation from family for up to eight hours. Bedtime for young families is either a fight or it is a foundation for positive family communication.

Some kindergartners were asked this question: what makes you feel you belong to your family? Most of them answered—bedtime! When the teacher probed more, the children talked about hugs and kisses and being tucked in and prayers and stories and promises. Bedtime in many, many homes is an enormous fight. It is a scolding or it is a spanking or it is a form of punishment. "Go to bed!" But, bedtime can be the foundation for a Christian family. Don't ignore that precious opportunity!

Today we added 250,000 children to this planet. That means one billion additional children will join us in the next ten years. But today, 3,500 children will become runaways or throwaways.

"When you get to your wits end, remember that God lives there." That old proverb helps stimulate me. For these are not just my children or your children but also, our children.

Rabbi Abraham Herschel pushes our corporate button: "We are not all equally guilty but we are equally responsible."

Aw, you say, "Dave, nice stuff, but too late. You're twenty-five years too late, Dave. Where were you twenty-five years ago when I needed that counsel?" It is never too late! It is never too late to rebuild a relationship with God or anyone else. It is never too late. Be careful! If you say it is too late, you are really denying the power of the Holy Spirit. You are denying the cross of Christ and its impact. It is never too late to rebuild a relationship.

Say, do you remember that earlier in this chapter I told you about that sign that was in the nursery? "The time to plant a tree was twenty-five years ago." But under it, there hung another line to that sign. It read, "The second-best time to plant a tree is today."

It is never too late to start over with your family. It is never too late to rebuild or build a relationship.

CHAPTER FIVE

Starting Over With Your Vocation

Exodus 3:1-12

The newspaper with the largest readership in America has no pictures. It has a few etchings. By the standards of many editors, *The Wall Street Journal* is depicted as the most accurate newspaper in America. It is published simultaneously in eighteen cities via satellite. *The Wall Street Journal* has a very high literary standard. It has won two Pulitzer prizes. *Fortune* magazine recently listed the top corporations in America. They listed Dow Jones, the publishers of *The Wall Street Journal*, as the top publishing organization in that field. I cannot help but wonder, how would *The Wall Street Journal* handle this story of Moses and the burning bush? How would they give it a headline? "Middle Manager Stumbles into Leadership Role." Or maybe this, "Sheepherder Discovers Spontaneous Combustion." Or maybe something like this, "From Bush-League Piety to Big-League Presidency." How about that?

Let's Start Over

What we know is that Moses worked for his father-in-law, Jethro. He tended the flocks. He was out there in the west side of the wilderness and I am sure, as far as Moses could see, it was an endless wilderness. A wasteland. No doubt he queries, "What am I going to do with my life? Is this all there is to it?" Suddenly, there was that burning bush! It intrigued him. He went over to see what it was. He had never seen anything like it before. It did not burn. It was not consumed. It became a compulsion for him. His curiosity got the best of him. Was it just a mirage out on the desert? And, yet, out of the bush came his name, "Moses, Moses." He nervously responded, "Here I am Lord." There was nothing God-forsaken about that wilderness. There was nothing God-forsaken about Moses. And there was certainly nothing God-forsaken about his profession.

Then God commands Moses to, "Take your sandals off. You are standing on holy ground. There is something rather spectacular to happen right here and now." He went on, "Moses, I want you to be the leader that frees my oppressed people in Egypt. Get them out of slavery. You're the one I want to handle the task."

That burning bush experience lit an unquenchable fire in the heart of Moses. Moses knew the bondage of slavery. Moses knew the oppression of the Egyptians and he could not stomach it! Thank God he jumped in to take on the challenge.

We have all been to campfires. There is so much beauty, joy, warmth, and good memories that float to the surface when you think about a campfire. But, when you look at a campfire the morning after, the warmth, light, joy, and the dancing shadows are all gone. There is nothing but the black, burnt wood and the ashes. It even smells stale. Nothing lovable about it. Nothing likable about it. In fact, it stinks! That is the way the people of Israel must have felt. All of the flame was gone. All of the hope, the joy, the love was out of it. It is no fun to be rich in a poor land. It is no fun to be poor in a rich land. It is no fun to be characterized as an oppressor in a world that is fed up with oppression. Moses had to feel all of those things. And the promise of God was, "I will be with you."

Moses went, speech impediment and all, to visit the Pharaoh. He fought the Pharaoh for the freedom of the people. Divine intervention through direct command and through devastating plagues did it! Finally, they won it. They won their freedom. Could it be that we are most open to the God of the burning bush when we find ourselves burned-out on our own competence, on our own skills, on ourselves? Maybe that is when we discover the God of the burning bush.

All of us experience little deaths. Many people fear death simply because they do not want to give up anything they love. To go alone through life without that love is a fearful thought. But, there are little deaths in life. The scholar that loses his memory, the ballerina that develops Parkinson's disease, the pitcher that loses his curve ball, the woman that discovers she cannot bear children, the manager that learns he has gone as far up that corporate ladder as he is ever going to go. There are little deaths. All of us want to leave our handprints and our footprints in the cement of somebody's Sunset Boulevard.

Let's Start Over

Does that bush still burn for us? Does that vision still have power to resurrect an ashen mind and spirit? Does God still speak to us? Does God still call us? Yes, I believe God does call us; through signs and symbols, through prophets and poets, through the one whose sandals knew the dusty roads of Palestine, through the one whose hands knew the nail prints, through the one whose hands did not come to damn, but came to bless. Ah, the bush still burns. Sometimes without the flamboyance and the fanfare. But, the bush still burns for us.

There is something within us that resonates to the gospel of Jesus Christ when we are told the story of his love and how he reaches out in mercy and forgiveness and says, I accept you. I am willing to forgive you. There is something that makes us respond to that. No manipulation in that love. No manipulation in that forgiveness. Friends, there is nothing you can do to get God to love you more or to love you less. His love for you is that perfect! His love for you is that consistent. Certainly that persistent. The love of God reaches out to heal your hurts, real and imagined—even healing for those hurts that you never deserved. The spirit of God works in the likes of you and me, so that it motivates us to pray, to give, to go, to be, to act in his name. What a privilege! That bush does still burn!

Martin Marty is a wonderful Christian historian. He is often quoted in popular publications. He is on the faculty of the University of Chicago. He honestly reflected, "Every time my friends succeed, I die a little." It is okay for strangers to succeed, but when friends succeed, it is hard to pray for their continued success. Why? Because we are all so human.

Starting Over With Your Vocation

How do we ordinary human beings, struggling to be faithful Christians, start over with our vocation? People are starting over with vocations today, particularly women in the middle years. Women are going back into the work place at an amazing pace. Today, 70% of women work outside the home. Women are pursuing education, maybe re-education, or just pursing a whole new goal in the area of education. Some women are pursuing voluntarism and making a career out of it. We know in our seminaries today, the students in the first year classes are averaging over thirty years of age. Many of them are pursuing a second career. People are starting over. There is the privilege of starting over for every one of us.

I have three suggestions for you on starting over with your vocation. Number one: Our vocation is really God's work entrusted into our hands. Everything you do whether it is teaching, coaching, preaching, managing, computing, directing, whatever it is you do, that is really a trust that God has placed in your hands. You have been given divine service responsibilities. When the choir comes to sing, they do not sing with less commitment for fifteen people than they do fifteen hundred. They sing to the glory of God. They do not do it just for the sake of performance. It is to offer the very best back to God. That is part of our mission, to offer everything that we do and have as a gift of thanksgiving to God. It is all part of the divine mission. We work not to acquire but to become. To become more Christlike.

A Presbyterian pastor was doing some research for a graduate degree. He was in Rochester, New York. He wanted to examine the marketplace and how right from wrong was discerned in the marketplace. One of the places he visited was a kosher meat market in Rochester, New York. He went into this kosher meat market and got acquainted with the owner of the store. He asked him what it was like to run a meat market. The owner of that store rose to the bait, "Well, let me tell you about Mrs. Solomon. Mrs. Solomon comes into my meat market and she asks for the best piece of meat available. That's all she wants. She doesn't care what it costs. She wants the best piece of meat available." But then he said, "Inevitably the next morning Mrs. Solomon will show up and she comes at the time when the crowd is the greatest and always announces to the crowd, 'That was the lousiest piece of meat I've ever put in my mouth, and you sold me that yesterday.' " He said, "You know she never tells it just to me, she tells it to everybody in the store." He said, "You can count on Mrs. Solomon going to one of the other five kosher meat markets in Rochester, New York for the next five weeks. She'll go elsewhere. But she'll eventually come back to my store." And he said, "And this is a classy store. We don't have prices on the meat. We figure if they want it, they're going to have to pay for it. So we don't publish our prices." But he said, "When I sell meat to Mrs. Solomon," he said, "I add ten cents at least per pound more." And he said, "I call that justice."

We are really not in our vocations for the sake of justice. We are in it as a sense of the divine mission, that there is something significant about what we are doing. I am a sucker for surveys. In *USA Today*, they always have some survey down in the lower left-hand corner. I am inevitably drawn to that. One survey read, "Who Do

People Respect?" They were really talking about professions. Right at the top of the list was the clergy. You knew I would point that out! The people surveyed said they respected the clergy because they had integrity. Right under them were pharmacists, then physicians, and then engineers. Guess what was at the very bottom? Used car salesmen.

But, then, they had another question. "Who does the business executive consult when in trouble?" Right at the top of the list was one's self and then one's spouse and then, third, legal counsel. Way down at the bottom of the list was the clergy. Somebody pointed out the contradiction and said, "How could that be?" You have got them on one list at the very top and on the other list at the very bottom. People said that they regard clergy as people with high integrity, but they just do not understand the marketplace. "They do not understand the jungle in which I work Monday through Friday." They cannot comprehend what it means to be torn between two symbols: the cross and the dollar bill. There are irreconcilable differences there that have to be dealt with up front.

A Presbyterian pastor in Pittsburgh asked a business executive, "Why do you attend church so faithfully?" With all seriousness he said, "I have more to confess than most people. I make many compromises in business and, at present, I see no way out."

What do you do to take a break from the pressure of your vocation? Do you ever truly rest? Do you manage your time well enough to provide some therapeutic periods? Do you ever allow yourself time for a vacation, meditation, prayer, or an afternoon nap? Do you ever go

71

out to lunch and note the beauty of the day and then decide to forget it and refuse to go back to your work that afternoon?

Rodney Hutson is an outstanding opthamologist with a very demanding practice. On Wednesdays, "Dr. Rodney" performs delicate surgical procedures under a microscope on patient's eyes. The tension is enormous. The pressure-cooker for him is the operating theater.

Late Wednesdays, Rodney heads for his farm near Tomball, Texas. He looks forward to Thursday when he can climb on his tractor and backhoe or on his bulldozer. To date, he has carved a four-acre lake out of the land. He enjoys doing it. He delights in handling that heavy machinery.

What a contrast Wednesdays are to Thursdays for him! He finds great release from the demands of delicate eye surgery by jumping on one of those "big cats" and moving earth, rocks, and trees without worrying about a slip of the scalpel.

The contrast is bold. The therapy is obvious.

What healing actions do you need to take to blow off some steam from your pressure-cooker?

June seems like the perfect month to slow down, sip something refreshing on the porch swing, and watch the days lengthen into spectacular sunsets. Wrong! Sociologist Keith Farrington, after measuring peoples' responses to thirty-one social indicators, says June is the most stressful month. Why? Because June includes for many people marriages, divorces, homes sold, vacations, and hospital admissions.

The next most stressful months by his measure are September and January. Most of us would have guessed

December. Farrington suggests that the stresses and strains of that holiday period are actually enjoyed by most people. We like to talk about how hectic December is but we do enjoy it. All that talk about the "demands of December" may actually be "folk myths."

Edward Farrell, in his book *Free To Be Nothing,* tells a wonderful story about Mother Teresa. Mother Teresa was walking through a crowd in Detroit when a woman remarked, "Her secret is that she is free to be nothing. Therefore, God can use her for anything."

How can I experience that? "Free to be nothing." I am constantly torn between my personal needs and the professional demands. Will you speak there? Can you help us raise some money? Surely you would like to serve on this national committee? I'm sorry to call you on your day off, but...

I struggle to find my balance in life. The requests, the expectations, the obligations, and the privileges threaten to swamp me at times. Without a significant effort to fight for some quiet time, I easily lose my sense of perspective. I need to focus on Jesus Christ and his claims and his will for my life. It is too easy to let everything get a little fuzzy.

God calls us to view our vocations as important entities of the divine mission.

Eli Black was chairman of the board and chief executive officer of United Foods. Several years ago, he locked the door of his office, took his attache case, and bashed out the window of his office. He threw himself through that window and plunged forty-four floors to his death on a street in Manhattan. Fifty-three years of age, at the top of his profession, he had all the success symbols. But something was missing. He and his company had been indicted for bribery of Honduran officials. He felt his troubles were more than he could handle. We need to view our vocation as divine mission.

The second point is, Christianity always questions the status quo. You want to start over with your vocation? You begin to question the status quo. I hear business people say all the time, "Business is business," as if business has a different ethic; as if business has a different set of rules. Business is business.

Your Nike shoes are put together in Indonesia. The components were made in the U.S.A. But laborers making 14 cents an hour assemble the shoes in Indonesia.

Somebody said, "Those unfortunate peasants don't know any better." But we do! We Bible-believing people have an obligation to connect the dots in life. Our faith demands we make those connections.

Part of the success of *Good Housekeeping* magazine is its ability to spot trends. Recently, to determine the trends in the 90's, *Good Housekeeping* hired Brainreserve, Inc. to make some observations on the 90's. One of their startling conclusions was this, "America is looking for something to believe in." To maintain the status quo is not the Christian's task. It is your obligation to question the status quo.

They tell me in the graduate schools of business around the country that the students are taught that Japan is the enemy. Japan is not the enemy. It is our own idolatry. It is our own love for the buck. It is our own greed. It is our own selfishness. Business is business. Friend, God does not call you to success. He calls you to be faithful to Jesus Christ. A Christian always questions the status quo. God loves you whether you make it to the winner's circle or whether you don't.

A teacher once remarked, "You know...my whole life I have been complaining that my work was constantly interrupted, until I discovered that my interruptions were my work." (Henri Nouwen) As Christians, God calls us to question the status quo.

The Herman Miller Furniture Manufacturing Company is highly respected in the industry. For many years, Max DePree served as Chairman and CEO. Before a meeting of his sixty to seventy officers and managers, he read a letter. It was a wonderful letter from a mother of one of his handicapped employees. It was a touching letter of gratitude. He almost got through the letter, but could not finish. Big boys do cry! He stood there tongue-tied, embarrassed, and unable to continue.

At that point, one of his senior vice presidents, Joe Schwartz—urbane, elegant, mature—strode up the center aisle, put his arm around his shoulder, kissed him on the cheek, and adjourned the meeting.

We need more of that kind of emotion in business. A Christian always questions the status quo.

The third point is really a question. Is your business your religion? Do you bow at the altar of business? Has business become so all-consuming for you that it has become your perspective in life? Let me ask you a question and this will help focus it.

Do you entertain people only to enhance your business contacts? Are you that pragmatic? If so, that can be awfully lonely. Or do you ever entertain simply to enhance a friendship? A wealthy person in this country is someone who has more than one friend. That is real wealth.

I cannot overemphasize the importance of the community of faith. For in the community of faith, we do have a sense of divine mission. We do question the status quo. We do ask the tough questions about what is on the altar of your religion. For in the community of faith, we have chosen to be vulnerable. We have chosen to take some risks. We have chosen to lower the masks that we wear Monday through Friday. For this is really the fellowship of the broken-hearted. We have broken God's heart. We have broken other people's hearts. That is what binds us together, that fellowship of the broken-hearted.

Malcolm Forbes, then chairman and editor-in-chief of *Forbes* magazine, was asked about the reason for his success. He came back with this surprising response, "ability, spelled i-n-h-e-r-i-t-a-n-c-e."

The *Forbes* magazine had been established by his father. Malcolm's financial security was well-founded. Malcolm had a choice to make: take it easy or work towards greater goals on the magazine. You know his choice. He started work at his desk at 6 a.m.

He has this insight for us, "Doing nothing is the hardest work of all...Retirement kills more people than hard work ever did."

At 9 p.m. every evening at Disney's Epcot in Orlando, they have something called "IllumiNations." The whole place stops for "IllumiNations." It is a dazzling, exciting, high-tech spectacle. It is amazing. Encircling the entire lake, there are lasers, lights, and fireworks. All of it is superbly synchronized to classical music. Magnificent! The sound system is powerful. The visual effects make your mouth drop open. Your mind can barely absorb all that goes on. I wondered about that program. I thought, how in the world does somebody sit down and figure all this out? Who does all this stuff? What kind of a creative mind is in back of that? It is genius at work! Then I read at the bottom of the program, "Sponsored by GE." The theme for the spectacle was "See the World in a New Light."

That is precisely what the church calls all of us to do; to see our vocations in a new light; to have a sense of calling.

Each generation has to learn the joy of giving. *Fortune* magazine had a cover story entitled, "How Much Should You Leave For Your Children?" How would you answer that? The magazine story talked about families where the children were left with substantial wealth. Many of these wealthy children went through an identity crisis. They really did not know who they were. They did not know what they were to do with all that had been given to them. Charity begins at home, but it does not end there! Don't ever forget that! Tolstoy said, "The vocation of every man and woman is to serve other people."

A missionary, John Mott, said, "To know a need and to have the capacity to meet it, constitutes a call." Florence Nightingale looked around her world and saw the filth, the corruption of the hospitals, and that was her call to nursing.

God does not call us to a task and then forsake us. God did not turn his back on Moses. He was an unlikely prospect as a leader. Yet, God chose him. Then, God strengthened him for the task. God embellished what talent he had and then turned it into something beautiful. Sure there were setbacks. Sure there were defeats. But, God does not call us to do a task and then abandon us. His word to Moses is a word for you and me, "I will not leave you."

CHAPTER SIX

Starting Over
With Your God

Acts 26:19-29

The petal pushers are ready. The petal pushers are always ready for the Valentine's Day outbreak of national affection. Five million Americans will buy roses for someone on Valentine's Day. Twenty-four thousand stems are sold per minute over a twenty-four hour period. That is a massive amount of roses. On average, you pay between five and six dollars a stem. Now if you are going to spend that kind of money, let me give you some practical advice. You can preserve those roses a little bit better if you will keep them out of bright sunlight and out of drafts. Some experts encourage you to nip about a half an inch off the stem when you first get them and use that little package of preservative that good florists always enclose, put it in the water, and your roses should last anywhere from four to ten days. No, the expression of your love in roses probably will not last beyond ten days. Only the sentiment will, but not the roses.

The Apostle Paul appeared before King Herod Agrippa. Herod Agrippa had all the power. He was in Caesarea to celebrate the success of the new governor, Festus. Paul was on his way to Rome to go on trial. King Herod Agrippa, the last of the unsavory dynasty of the Herods, the hated Herods, granted Paul a preliminary hearing in Caesarea.

Everything that you ever imagined, just like the movies, was true. Opulence prevailed. The gold, the marble and the pillars, it was all real. It was prestigious. It was elegant. It was show business. It was an opportunity to display pomp and power. Just imagine, seated high on that marble throne, several levels above anyone else, King Herod Agrippa. The flowing royal purple robes—oh, what a sight! Off to his right, at a lower level, is the governor in his scarlet robes, Festus. Gathered around them were the captains, the legion-naires, and the centurions. All gathered in precise military formation and at attention. It was a somber display of authority. It was intimidating. In that imposing setting, you have a very unimposing individual down there at floor level. A little wisp of a guy who was not a threat to anybody. Physically, he did not look like much. He had been beaten many times. There was nothing about his stature that was impressive. He was standing there constrained by chains. Nobody was afraid of him. The "Hall of Audience" built by Herod the Great was quiet. This was the opportunity to hear from this changed man in chains, the Apostle Paul.

Paul began to recount to King Herod Agrippa and Festus his experiences. He explained how, on the road to Damascus, he was on his way to persecute Christians. An intellectual, a well-educated Jew, a Roman citizen on his way to destroy what he thought was the enemy of Judaism, Christianity. Suddenly, he was arrested. No, not by some soldiers. A divine encounter took place. He said the risen Christ confronted him. In a flash, he knew that this was the Messiah. The sight was so great that it temporarily blinded Paul. Question: in the "Hall of Audience," who do you think really was on trial? Was it Paul? Was it Christianity? Was it Festus? Was it King Herod Agrippa?

Paul saw this moment as an opportunity to cut loose in terms of his proclamation of the Gospel. He explained the purpose of the Crucifixion and the Resurrection, and the fulfillment of the Old Testament scriptures and prophecy. But, as he cut loose on his witness to the Gospel, a loud voice cut him off. The Greek suggests more than just a loud voice. It means with "great emotion." The source of the great emotion was the governor, Festus. Festus shouts, "Paul, Paul, you are mad; your great learning has made you mad."

It was magnificent madness. It was a kind of magnificent madness for which we long in this world. It was the kind of magnificent madness that enabled Paul to feel like he was part of a great redemptive parade down through history. It was the kind of magnificent madness that enabled Paul to feel like he had been forgiven for his persecution of Christians years earlier. It was the kind of magnificent madness that enabled Paul to experience healing from the deadly snake bite on the Isle of Patmos.

This man was different. He knew sin. He knew despair. Now, God's grace had made him right in Jesus Christ. Now, Paul was at peace in the presence of these powerful Romans, Festus and Agrippa. "Paul, you are mad; your learning has made you mad."

What Paul had discovered was a totally new focus for his perspective on life. A new center for his being. Jesus Christ determined that focus. Festus simply had a misdiagnosis on his hands. Paul was not some kind of manic-depressive. What he had in Paul was authentic joy that has its source in Jesus Christ. When that confrontation took place, it did not throw Paul off track. He forged ahead and replied, "No, I'm not mad. I'm telling you the sober truth." Then, it was time for King Herod Agrippa to respond, "Almost, Paul, almost thou persuadest me to be a Christian." (K.J.V.) Almost! Close! Close! But close doesn't count! Certainly not in the Kingdom of God.

"Almost thou persuadest me to be a Christian." That is one of the saddest statements in Scripture. Why? Because it is the last remembrance we have of the Herods. It is the last statement recorded in history of the dynasty of the hated Herods. Almost! "Almost thou persuadest me to be a Christian."

There is special poignancy in that response. For in that response, we always feel like if only Paul had been a little bit more eloquent, maybe, just maybe, King Herod Agrippa might have changed all of history. If only King Herod had been just a little bit more responsive. If only, if only! "Almost thou persuadest me to be a Christian." Sad, isn't it?

The caddy watched as the frustrated golfer threw his three wood in the pond. Dissatisfied, he threw all of his woods in the pond. Still not pacified, he threw all of his irons in the pond.

The golfer turned to his caddy and said, "Now, I'm going to throw myself in that pond and drown myself."

The caddy predicted, "You'll never do it!" The golfer reacted, "What did you just say?" The caddy said, "You'll never do it! You'll never drown yourself in that pond!"

The golfer yelled, "Why?"

The caddy replied, "Because you can't keep your head down."

Almost is not good enough!

"In the absence of any other proof, the thumb alone would convince me of God's existence." That insight from Sir Isaac Newton is a hint that almost is not good enough.

Did you ever play hide and seek as a kid? It was so much fun. As kids, we could spend hours with hide and seek. Remember how there was always one kid in the group that did a better job of hiding than everybody else? That kid would manage to hide so well that nobody would ever find him. So, the rest of the crowd would finally give up and they would say "Aw, let him rot! Let him rot! We'll just go on and we'll start another game. Let's go back to home base and we'll start all over." A little while later, the kid that was so good at hiding would finally emerge out of the bushes. He would casually amble over to home base and say, "Hey, why didn't somebody find me? I thought we were playing hide and seek, not hide and let's quit."

Do adults play hide and seek? We hide our feelings, our emotions, our real thoughts from one another. We try to hide from God. Yet, what we really want is someone to find us. We want somebody to seek us out. And when someone finds us, we are really not sure what to do. Also, there really is no place to hide. Oh, we try. We hide behind our affluence, our work, our leisure, and our business. But really, where do we hide?

Do you remember how exciting it was when you found somebody? You would surprise them in their hideout. They would jump out! Somebody would be scared. They would yell! They would scream! They would laugh! They would run! The ecstasy of it all. Could that be how God feels about us? The Bible says there is rejoicing in heaven over one sinner that repents. Could it be that God feels that way about you and me? Maybe that is why starting over with God is so important. Because we get the opportunity to experience something of the substance of that magnificent madness of which Paul was accused.

How do you start over with your God? "...Repent and turn to God and perform deeds worthy of... repentance." (Acts 26:20).

First, you repent. The Greek really means to change your mind.

In a Confirmation Class, the teenage students were asked to complete this sentence and illustrate.

"The church is like a _____."

Starting Over With Your God

One answer read, "The church is like a ski resort.
It is warm inside.
Some folks like the sitting around part best.
You need help to get to the top.
It is dead in summer.
It is only fun during certain seasons of the
year.
You risk a lot of pain and brokenness."
There is repentance on the ski slopes. Did you know
that? In skiing, you move with the flow of the terrain.
The terrain is a friend. When you try to counter the
terrain, fight it or plow through it, you are the one that
is going to give. You pay the price usually by wiping out.
When you feel like you are losing it, that is when you
need to snowplow or find your hockey stop so you can
repent, reorganize, get reoriented, get under control, and
in rhythm with the terrain. U turns are necessary in life.
Repentance is a biblical invitation. "U turns permitted."
Repentance packs a wallop! It has an economic, social,
educational, and spiritual impact.

You have the power to change your mind. You have
the power to make a difference. You have knowledge,
will, and emotions as part of your psyche. Repentance is
an act of the will. You decide to do something different
with your life. You decide that what you are doing is not
right. It is wrong. It is sin. It is detrimental to your well-
being. You stop. You adopt a whole new set of values:
values centered in the teachings of Jesus Christ. Oh yes,
you are sorry for the past. Of course. But, God's grace
enables you to start all over again, to begin again. Even
though God has meant nothing to you in the past,
suddenly, God becomes everything to you. That is the

beauty of repentance. It is an experience in mercy. The mercy shown sinners in Jesus Christ. If you are going to start over, you have to start with repentance. Your journey from despair to hope begins with repentance. God not only suffered and died for our sins, but also promised to remember our sins no more. Never bring it up again!

The second thing you do to start over with God is to change your quality of life. Your action has to complement your repentance. It does not work any other way.

Dennis Conner, winner of the America's Cup, wrote a book entitled *The Art of Winning.* In it he says, "The America's Cup is now much more than a sailboat race. It's about 15% sailing—and the rest is preparation, design, planning, fund-raising, committee work, training, building a team, logistics and management."

And I thought it was just a race involving some wealthy sailors. What Conner describes is not sailing. It is life!

Following Jesus Christ is not an extracurricular activity. It is not just one course you choose from a whole group of electives. It is life! Two-thirds of Americans never give any time to community activities. We have no real heroes. One-third of Americans have never contributed to any charitable cause. According to *Business Week,* June 3, 1991, the saddest finding is that 50% of J. Walter Thompson's respondents say that nobody really knows them. Maybe the college slang is right, "Get a life!" You can in Christ.

Some of us have prayed the same prayer of confession during the worship, both corporate and personal, week in and week out. Do you realize that really is not repentance? That is hypocrisy. How come? Because you really do not intend to change. To say that same prayer of confession, week after week, and assume that God covers you without any intention to reform is to depend on liturgy for salvation. That will never make it! Christ introduces us to a completely new set of values. Laws do not govern that change. Love governs that change. It is the magnetism of God's love that draws you to the mercy of the cross. No matter how many dozen roses, they can never adequately express that kind of love. Its source has to be divine. But, the laws stay the same. God's law does not break you. Oh, you may break the laws of God, but the law stays the same. You are the one who ends up broken on them. The heart of God breaks when you sin. But, God draws you back in relationship. God longs for a relationship with you. God's bridge over the great gulf in your relationship is Jesus Christ. I ask you, when and where do you really want God to do something significant in your life? Think about that. Until you ask that question of yourself, your quality of life never proves to be fulfilling. Nor will you experience God's peace. That question deserves to be on your daily agenda.

Twice in the New Testament, Jesus makes a reference to sparrows—once in Matthew and the other in Luke. In Matthew, it says for a penny you can buy two sparrows. Sparrows were a cheap offering. More than that, most viewed sparrows as a cheap source of food. Sparrows, of course, are plentiful all over the world. They chatter. They quarrel. They are noisy. They mess up your chimney. Sparrows were everywhere. In Luke, we learn that for two pennies you not only could get four sparrows, but you could get a fifth. They threw in an extra. It did not cost anything. It is a lagniappe experience. It is the thirteenth donut when you buy a dozen. It is so cheap, they just throw an extra one in for you. The Scripture solemnly suggests "and not one of them is forgotten before God." Then Luke and Matthew both add, "Fear not, you are of much more value than many sparrows." To follow Jesus Christ is not to withdraw from life but to engage life. God does not call you to an insecure life, lacking reason, logic or euphoria. God calls you to a pilgrimage with Christ.

No matter what you say about India, it is not an exaggeration. Fifteen percent of the world's population is in India. In one-third of the space of the U.S.A., three times our population lives there, 850 million people. It is the world's largest democracy and one of our neediest countries physically and spiritually. Every day, 55,000 children are born. Eight percent of their inhabitants live in villages.

I visited numerous villages in India. What a challenge to the power of the Gospel of Jesus Christ! Dominated by Hinduism, the darkness is all-pervasive. Mission India is penetrating that country with the message of hope. They do it through literacy. Much of the printed tools they use carry the biblical message. When villagers turn to Christ, they begin to care for each other, women and children included, and visibly change in terms of their optimism. Christianity is the power of light over darkness. I saw it! The promised power of the Gospel is not empty.

Our quality of life makes a statement. We need to wrap the bones of our faith in living flesh, the living Christ.

Starting Over With Your God

How do you get there? Repent. Then, change your life-style. It is that simple. It is an act of the will. By the enabling power of the Holy Spirit, you can act by faith, accept the love of Jesus Christ, and start over with your God.

CHAPTER SEVEN

Starting Over
With Your Empty Nest

Psalm 16:5-11

Franz Schubert put it best when he said, "I'd rather lead a life of uncertainty and poverty than one of drudgery." When you drive your youngest child to college, get him or her settled in the dormitory for the fall semester, then kiss and hug for that final goodbye, the empty nest looms large! When you finally get home, it shocks you to discover that no longer do you need to purchase soft drinks in twelve packs, do laundry daily, prepare full meals and plenty of cookies for snacks, fight for the TV remote control or ask someone to "turn that music down!"

For years, you have invested yourself in nurturing, teaching, and serving others. In fact, the first half of your life has been essentially that: nurturing, chauffeuring, coaching, cheering, counseling, serving family members, and even caring for others in the community through volunteer organizations.

Probably, the second half of your life has just begun. For women, losing the power of procreation forces her to redirect her energies. At whatever age a woman determines that she will not have another child, an intriguing phenomenon takes place. She generates a new kind of creativity. Suddenly, she has the opportunity to pour herself into a new pursuit.

In her late forties, Pene is an intelligent, engaging, articulate woman. Her husband is a physician. Economically, she is secure. She has seen her last child off to college. As we walked to a meeting through a parking garage in Louisville, I asked her about her personal experience with the empty nest. She spoke of missing her kids, spending plenty of money on telephone calls and planning future vacations and visits to the campus. But at home, she found loneliness.

Two weeks after Pene dropped her son off at Duke University, she called to see if he needed a care package.

His response was, "Yeah, please send my hair dryer and brush!"

In fear, his concerned mother asked, "What have you been doing with your hair?"

The creative, carefree freshman replied, "I've just been wearing my hat."

Her husband's career immersed him. He cared for her. There was no question about their love. However, she said that with the children gone, there were wonderful romantic moments. Plenty of freedom. But, there were also long stretches of silence. She could stand it no longer. Her creative juices needed a new outlet. She took a job as a travel agent. She quickly pointed out that this could not hurt her marriage, but rather enhance it.

She now felt like she was using some of her creative skills in a positive fashion.

In truth, sometimes we love the empty nest and other times we hate it. The marital relationship always has some ambivalence in the mix. It may well force us to rebuild relationships that we have long ignored. Oh, maybe not ignored, but a least taken for granted.

This is a time for partners to transcend dependency and relish self-declaration. Children have become adults. Economic freedom allows for new adventures. This is not the time that marriages characteristically break up. The teen years and about age thirty are the high-water marks for divorce. Middle age couples tend to separate. The separation may not be geographical. It more often is emotional. But, the empty nest can also serve to stimulate individual growth or at least to do a neat assessment.

USA Today reported on an eight year study that shows most parents are happier with their marriages after the last child leaves home.

Lynn White, a sociologist at the University of Nebraska, interviewed four hundred and two parents in 1983 when at least one child, 14 or older, was still at home and again in 1988.

Her conclusion: "When the last kid leaves home, the marriage improves. It may even experience a brief mini-honeymoon."

Why? Probably because the two have more free time and more time together. Just having others in the household, no matter how much they are loved, interferes with the couples' one-on-one relationship.

Starting Over With Your Empty Nest

Not all mothers pine when their children depart. In fact, many experience relief. Kids leaving home will not make a lousy marriage wonderful. But, it may provide the opportunity for some improvement.

Please note that continued parental well-being depends on consistent contact with the children. Sociologist White said, "Ninety percent of those we interviewed have talked to a child the previous day. Life's satisfaction declines if they're not in regular touch."

An English teacher received this blooper from one of her students: "Socrates was a famous Greek teacher who went around giving people advice. They killed him. Socrates died from an overdose of wedlock." That will do it to you every time! Hemlock is equally dangerous.

I am a student of statistics, particularly statistics that shape our lives. According to a Roper report poll of 1,994 adults, the five most romantic gestures are a weekend get-away, long-stemmed roses, a candlelight dinner at a restaurant, other flowers, or a love letter.

It is at the point of the empty nest that many people choose to start over. Psalm 16 is so relevant! "Show me that path of life." The empty nest is a new path. How do we see that path as part of our spiritual pilgrimage?

Often, a woman at this stage in life looks for replenishment of purpose for the second half of her life. She chooses to cultivate talents half-finished. She permits ambitions once sidetracked to now take the forefront of her interest. She becomes aggressive in the service of her own convictions rather than function as a passive-aggressive person to accommodate her family.

Let's Start Over

Some women seek employment outside the home for the first time. She decides to pursue a post-graduate degree in a field that has taken on new interest for her. She reflects on her gifts of the Spirit. Rather than allowing the empty nest syndrome to drive her into depression, she invests her creativity, intelligence, and energy into a new opportunity. It is not that raising a family has diminished her self-esteem, but rather, it is an opportunity for the enhancement of her self-esteem in a whole new arena.

My wife, Linda, has always been employed outside the home as a musician. In fact, while I was a student at the University of Edinburgh in Scotland, Linda was Minister of Music at First Presbyterian Church in Flushing, New York. As organist, she conducted the choir from the console. She was vibrant and creative. They loved her. They did not want to lose her. They knew that Linda and I planned to be married. They hoped I would choose to continue my seminary education in the New York City area so Linda would continue on their staff. Fearing that she might marry me and move elsewhere, they hired me, sight unseen!! I was to be Student Assistant. Obviously, she got me my first job. She enjoys telling that story. But, it is also true. They needed her more than they needed me.

As the empty nest became a reality for us, with Sheri in college and Peter a recent college graduate, Linda invested herself even more intensely in her music. Composing, arranging, conducting, and accompanying were her primary interest.

Now, she turned up the intensity a notch.

Recording her piano music became a new creative outlet. To date, she has completed six recordings displaying her keyboard artistry. They are unique blendings of gospel music with classical themes. Some are accompanied by synthesizer and some by full orchestra. It is true that she has received some notoriety through them. This is well-deserved. She has incredible talent. Her creativity is just amazing. I know. I hear her work at it on a daily basis. Often, at midnight, she will get an inspiration and head for the keyboard.

Creativity knows no schedule.

These recordings have given her a new sense of self-esteem. This is the way Linda has handled the empty nest. It fascinates me that these recordings have transpired precisely at the time when the empty nest became a reality.

I have talked of some women at this stage in life, but what of men? Often in mid-life, men depart from their traditional patterns. They may have been extremely conservative in terms of economics. Now, they decide to spend some money and try something different. They start to take some chances. Some live on the edge of risk; snow skiing, bicycling through New England, white water rafting, backpacking in the wilderness, off-road motorcycling, or running for political office. Some change hairstyles, cars, and clothes.

Often, what men discover is that management does not automatically promote good old boys. Sometimes they get fired. Their employment is not secure. Identity does not increase necessarily as one climbs the corporate ladder. Happiness is not an automatic dividend from one's vocation. Safety does not always come through financial security. Some choose to jump from their profession into running a boutique. Some choose to sail the Caribbean. Some choose to plant a garden for which they have always longed. Often, it is a decision to sell the big house. No longer do they need substantial space for just two adults. In fact, it has become downright embarrassing because that home ties up male identity. With apologies to wives who are equally important as providers, it represents a display of all that he has accomplished, the sum of his life's work. It may be his only asset. But now, he is ready to make a break. He chooses to move into more modest space. He seeks refreshment in less stereotyped ways. Gratification comes in a variety of forms. It is refreshing to discover that it does not only come through the marketplace. One man said, "I find that every time I get on a Board, I become President. I was running down like an old clock."

You should greet change as a friend. The future is effervescent with possibilities. Maybe now is the time for travel. Maybe now success can take on a new definition. In a deeper sense, one discovers that risk is exciting at middle age.

You can be replenished. There really ought to be an award for people who come to understand the concept of "enough." Good enough. Successful enough. Thin enough. Rich enough. Socially responsible enough. When you have self-respect, you have enough; and when you have enough, you have self-respect. Fortunately, there are always enough people and events around us to stretch us. We do not have to worry about falling into the self-satisfied ditches of "absolute" maturity.

I have a number of friends who choose, at middle age, to go to work for non-profit organizations. A food bank, a home for the mentally handicapped, a hospital, a missionary service, a home for children taken from abusive situations, a soup kitchen—the list seems infinite. In these opportunities, they have realized new shades of the rainbow of fulfillment. George Gallup, Jr. says we annually give 20 billion volunteer hours and often more.

Anytime you move from certainty to uncertainty, there is pain. But, there is also excitement. All of us need to flirt with the edge of adventure. Taking a risk can be fun. Maybe that is what Jesus meant in John 10:10 when he said, "I came that you might have life and that more abundantly."

The eagle gently coaxes offspring to the edge of the nest. The eaglet resists her persistent nudging. "Why does the thrill of soaring have to begin with the fear of falling?" The push was the remaining parental obligation. The fear of falling had to be conquered to thrill to the joy of soaring. The greatest gift of the eagle is the push. Without the push, the privilege of being an eagle would not be understood. One by one, the eagle pushed them out of the nest and they flew!

If we do not change, we choose not to grow. If we do not grow, we are not really living. Any growth with which I am familiar demands a temporary surrender of security. You break familiar patterns. The safety nets are not always there. Dostoevsky put it, "Taking a new step, uttering a new word, is what people fear most." The real fear should be of the opposite course.

Part of our problem in Western civilization is that we worship youth. When that happens, we deny ourselves any sense of fulfillment beyond youth. Beyond youth, there is much more than just dull experience. There has to be more to rival the accumulation of goods and success. If not, then we trap ourselves into stale and repetitious middle age. The fastest growing segment of our population in America is the over fifty age group. In this decade, there will be more people over sixty-five than teenagers.

For the Christian, the delights of self-discovery are always available. That is the value of the gifts of the Holy Spirit. God has promised us new dimensions of discovery. God enhances our capacity for love and fulfillment. Isaiah reminds us, "Behold I am doing a new thing. Can you not perceive it?"

What new gift do you feel the Holy Spirit has for you at middle age? I believe that is a question worth pondering. Fascinating, isn't it, that the Bible never ties the gifts of the Spirit to genetics, ethnicity, sexual identity, or age. God does not tie the fruit of the Spirit— "love, joy, peace, patience, kindness, goodness, faithfulness, gentleness and self-control"—to any age or stage in life.

Comedienne Lily Tomlin quipped, "If I'd known what it would be like to have it all, I might have settled for less."

Sitting across the aisle from me on an airplane was a huge man. We talked about the empty nest. He said he had just taken his third son, last child, to college. He said he really couldn't explain it, but as he left that boy off at college to fulfill his dream on a full soccer scholarship, he drove home alone and cried. He said the tears truly flowed. At times, he could not see well enough to continue driving. He had to pull off the road and try to regain his composure. His grief was overwhelming. The sense of loss was real. There seemed to be something terminal about this separation.

As he reflected back on the experience, he related to me that he had a unique insight. All through his son's high school years, the father was driven, successful, and extremely busy. Having dropped his son off at college, he suddenly realized that in four years of high school all he had ever seen of his son's athletic ability in soccer was one quarter of one game!

Sad! Regrets? Of course there are regrets. However, we do not live pointed toward the past. By God's grace, we point to the future. The label, "the middle age crazies," does not have to be your experience. You are a gifted person. God's Spirit wants to fill you and use you in some unique capacity. So, the first half of your life is over. Now what? How would you like God to use you in the second half? I dare you to ask God for some direction in this area. If you do, I dare to believe you are in for a fascinating trip. In it, you will discover the abundant life promised in John 10. As the Psalmist put it, "fullness of joy" and "pleasures forevermore." That is your legacy.

CHAPTER EIGHT

Starting Over With Your Frustrations

Colossians 3:12-17

Frustration is a daily experience. What frustrates you? Balancing your checkbook, traffic jams, surly sales clerks, being put on hold, people that don't listen, or keys that break off in the lock?

God's word counsels us to be patient. But is patience overrated? Yogi Berra, the famed Yankee catcher, once said, "I don't want to make the wrong mistake!"

Forty-seven year old Kathy had just given birth to her fifth child. The first morning she was home after the delivery, everything was in chaos. The baby was screaming, the other children were demanding some attention, and her stitches were hurting.

Her seven-year old reminded her that, "Today is the Mothers' Tea at school."

Kathy said, "I couldn't possibly go. My daughter Jenny put her hands on her hips and admonished: 'If you can't be there for me, why are you having more children?' I bundled up my newborn, squeezed into my dress and went."

Our frustrations demand patience.

If patience is just a passive attitude, then it is over-rated.

In Colossians 3:12, the insightful Apostle Paul wrote, "Put on then, as God's chosen ones, holy and beloved, compassion, kindness, lowly, meekness and patience..." Paul propounds that we are to strip off some of our old characteristics and put on some new ones. Paul suggests to you that when you become a Christian, a new person in Christ, you ought to make some changes. These changes profoundly affect personality, perspective, and life-style.

Change is a constant. We live in a dynamic crucible called life. Christian discipleship is continual and pro-gressive. You are in a process of becoming more Christ-like.

When a person is serious about tuning life to the song of salvation, barriers begin to break down. Barriers like birth, nationality, culture, ritual, class—all begin to disintegrate. When God's Spirit changes you, according to Colossians 3:12, you take on some new titles such as, "chosen ones, holy, and beloved." But wait a minute! Only the Jews could carry the title "Chosen Ones." That is correct! However, Paul is now suggesting that, as Christians, we are the children of promise! These precious titles now belong to Christians.

Patience is not generally affirmed in our culture. We are much more familiar with instant gratification. We are conditioned to expect immediate payoffs. Is that God's plan? No. The world's recommendation of instant gratification will never allow you to build a business, marriage, a relationship with your children or grand-children, a body, a bank account or a walk with God.

Scott Peck in *The Road Less Traveled* summed it up for me, "Delaying gratification is a process of scheduling the pain and pleasure in life in such a way as to enhance the pleasure by meeting and experiencing the pain first and getting it over with...it is the only decent way to live."

Our frustrations flow out of who we are and whose we are. We dare not separate body, mind, and spirit. You cannot separate being and doing. I Peter 2:10 counsels, "Once you were no people but now you are God's people. Once you had not received mercy but now you have received mercy."

We use the word metamorphosis to describe the transitional state of the caterpillar becoming a butterfly. To be in a metamorphic state implies that the insect is in a state of becoming. As Christians, we are too! We are in a state of becoming.

Here is a tough question. Who loves you? Of the people who love you, who loves you the most? No matter your answer to those two tough questions, the love you have experienced pales next to the love that God extends to us in Jesus Christ. God's love is persistent. God's love is a constant. God's love is a kiss of grace. It is the love of God that provides the driving force, the strength, the patience that you need to deal with your frustrations on a daily basis. You cannot handle it on your own. You need a source of strength beyond your own power.

Starting Over With Your Frustrations

Back to the Apostle Paul. He suggests that we "put on then" the garments of Christian grace. There are some things that you can add to your character. It is your move. You can ask God for patience. New coverage.

What is patience anyway? Someone has said, "Patience is the refusal to be upset by perverse people."

The Bible invites us to ask the Holy Spirit for specific gifts. One of the things that I have to ask for over and over is to remain whole and triumphant even in the down times. Yes, as a pastor, I too have down times. When is life toughest for me? Always at the point of patience. Patience in terms of relationships. There are times in my life when hurts and rejections sap my energy, when my human strengths are spent, and all the natural juices have been drained from me. It is then that I need God's gift of patience.

Our Savior taught us what it means to be patient. He was patient with the Pharisees, patient with the persecutors, and patient with his disciples. Patience is real. It is observable. There is nothing superficial about it. There is nothing subjective about it. It has concrete overtones. One of the blessings that Jesus taught us is that you cannot separate being and doing. When you reflect on that trial and crucifixion of Jesus, his patience has to amaze you. They spit on him, ridiculed him, beat him, mocked him, and crucified him. Nowhere is there a hint of bitterness, cynicism, or despair. There is a divine element to patience. The patience of God persists. Divine patience puts up with us, with our anger, with our sinning, and with our whining. Never, never can we separate ourselves from the love of God. Never does

God cast us aside. Never does he throw us overboard. Always, God draws us back to his mercy and patience.

Frustrating traffic jams face anyone who lives in a large metropolitan center. I have come to appreciate patience in the midst of the traffic jams in Houston. Patience is something you admire in the driver behind you, but do not understand in the driver ahead of you.

I greeted one of my staff members one morning with a question, "How are you doing?" She answered by saying she identified with a bumper sticker she had just seen. It read, "Heaven doesn't want me and Hell is afraid I'll take over."

The world does not generally perceive we Americans as patient people. Ask a European. Ask a Russian who knows what it is to stand in line for everything from drugstore items to Big Macs. We change cars, houses, jobs, and spouses with an ease and rapidity that shocks the rest of the world. We Americans are not a patient people. Have you noticed this? You never realize how patient you can be until the person who is arguing with you happens to be your boss.

Candidly, I have a difficult time being patient with the committee process. Yes, I believe in the process. Sadly, my patience at committee meetings often runs thin. George Will captured the essence of my feelings. The author and pundit said of football, "It combines the two worst things about American life. It is violence punctuated by committee meetings."

Patience is a Christian virtue. The Apostle Paul rated it "a fruit of the Spirit." St. Augustine called it, "the companion of wisdom." We say the ultimate provocation is proverbially "enough to try the patience of a saint."

Starting Over With Your Frustrations

In his book entitled *Oh, The Places You Go!*, Dr. Seuss reminds us: "Remember that Life's a Great Balancing Act." He urges: "On you will go though the weather be foul. On you will go though your enemies prowl...onward up many a frightening creek, though your arms may get sore and your sneakers may leak...And will you succeed? Yes! You will, indeed! [ninety-eight and three quarters guaranteed.]" Even Dr. Seuss understands our need for and our inclination against patience.

The biblical standard for patience is not passive resignation, but purposeful action toward a long-range goal. "Patience is accepting a difficult situation without giving God a deadline to remove it."

It generally takes plain, simple, unappetizing patience to achieve a business goal. The overnight fortune is a myth!

The corporate world knows something of patience. Gillette's light weight, laser-welded razor took thirteen years, twenty-two patent applications, and two hundred millon dollars to bring it to market. Gillette has forty engineers, metallurgists, and physicists at their British research facility spending their days thinking about shaving and little else. In 1977, one of them had a bright idea. John Francis had already figured out how to create a thinner razor blade that would make Gillette's cartridges easier to clean. Then, the design engineer remembered a notion he had toyed with for years: he could set the thinner blades on springs so that they would follow the contours of the face or body. It turned out to be a great idea. The high-tech Sensor razor came face to face with five million new faces in its first month on the market. Patience won the day for Gillette.

Let's Start Over

Aldous Huxley said, "Waiting is torture." I would add to that, waiting is torture only without a goal in sight. Why is it that grandmothers and grandfathers seem to have more patience than the rest of us? Grandmother and grandfather had just kept the grandchildren, ages 4 and 6, while their daughter and son-in-law went on a lovely European vacation. The task of caring for the grandchildren was taxing. In fact, it was downright exhausting.

At the end of the two week period, the parents came to pick up their children. When the grandchildren and their parents were in the automobile and everything was packed, they started backing out of the driveway. The grandparents were out on the lawn blowing kisses and waving goodbye. Suddenly, grandmother muttered to grandfather, "They just drove over my foot, but keep right on smiling and waving!"

The good news is that God is patient with you. God is not finished with you yet. "He who began a good work in you will bring it to completion in the day of Jesus Christ." [Philippians 1:6]. You can trust Jesus Christ. You can trust the power of the Holy Spirit. You can trust God's resources to see you through life's breaking points. There are times in life when we feel like quitting. It is at that point that you can experience something of God's resources to deal with your frustrations.

It is always easier to quit than it is to be patient. In his book, *Who You Are When No One's Looking,* Bill Hybels asked a tough question: "Looking back over the last ten years of your life, what do you wish you had not quit?"

Starting Over With Your Frustrations

How would you answer that? High school, college, graduate school, dance lessons, tennis lessons, piano lessons, a relationship, a friendship, a position that had potential for advancement, the church? Many of us live with scars of lingering wounds for having quit on something or someone. We shake our heads and ask ourselves, "Why did I cash in so early? If I had just been more patient maybe I could have..."

It is always easier to quit than to be patient. It is always easier to watch TV after work than to take additional courses at a local community college. It is always easier to go outside and play than to practice the scales on the piano. It is always easier to storm out of a room during an argument than to stay and work through the conflict. It is always easier to read the paper and drink coffee in your bathrobe than get yourself and your family up, dressed, and ready to go to church on Sunday morning. It is always easier to do what you want with your life than to kneel before God, turn the controls over to him and wait patiently, expectantly and even agonizingly for God to guide you. It is infinitely easier to quit than to be patient.

How do we gain patience? Hybels helped me when he taught that I must crash through life's quitting points. I have played soccer, hockey, and football at competitive levels. I know what it is as an athlete to have to do windsprints—to run when your sides were splitting, your legs feel like logs, your throat is on fire, and your mind is screaming at you "Quit! Quit!" I know what it is to argue with my wife. Yes, we do have disagreements. Sometimes we argue over the same thing, an item we have covered seemingly hundreds of times before. All it takes is that one angry magic word to ignite the fireworks. Everything seems to scream at you "Quit! Quit!" I know what it is to struggle with my own character. To wrestle with a particular tendency or sin. I know what it is to struggle with someone who makes light of your morals. I know what it is to struggle with God when the Holy Spirit is working on me, demanding important changes and redirecting my thinking. There are enormous demands on us. Sometimes, we feel incredibly lonely. "Nobody else is doing this."

A young woman returned from her university on Spring Break and said to her mother, "I must be the only virgin at my university." She wasn't. But, she sure felt like it. There are quitting points in life, but the patience God has promised to us by the power of the Holy Spirit enables us to crash through life's quitting points.

In our culture, people often praise quitting. There is kind of a sweet relief to cashing in. I insist that quitting is not glamorous.

What is your quitting point? I challenge you, whatever your quitting point appears to be, to test God's faithfulness. Go ahead and press the truth of God's word. Take the risk and pray, "God, I am going to trust you to give me the patience, the strength, and the wisdom to crash through this quitting point."

If you do, I promise that God will bring you out on the other side of that quitting point in one piece. When that happens, you will make a wonderful discovery. The quitting point is not made of steel, but of tissue paper.

You can go through it. Quitting points are painful. Jesus patiently accepted the cross when all hell screamed out, "Quit! Quit!" Your quitting point is not made of steel, but of tissue paper. You can crash through. You will come out in one piece on the other side. God's patience is sufficient for your frustration. It is your gift to claim.

Whenever my frustrations are overwhelming, I rest on the test of Hebrews 12:2, "Who for the joy that was beset before him endured the cross..." Christ did that for you. You are that important to God!

Nature teaches us that the chrysanthemums come to flower in the fall of the year. The same is true in your life. We are constantly in a state of becoming, of meta-morphosis, as the caterpillar changes into a butterfly. You assimilate, love, disappoint, hurt, and succeed. But this process brings you to bloom. God's patience is an act of power. You can advance in God's plan. You can face the fruit of your own experience, investigation, and choice.

How does God capture your attention? Not by threats of judgment. Not by the penalty of pain. Not by the temperature of hell. Not by the atmosphere of heaven. But by his incredible goodness and patience. He chose not to win us from a throne, but from a cross.

The Apostle Paul was a blasphemer of Christ and his church. He often flung hot, angry words at Christians accusing them of crimes against God. The Bible portrays him as insolvent and violent. At times, he must have been an arrogant sadist—inflicting pain for the sheer, sick joy of it on Christians. He calls himself, "The chief of sinners." Paul never could escape from his memories. He could never forget that he was a sinner; but equally, he could never forget that he was a forgiven sinner. So are you! Claim it in the name of Christ.

CHAPTER NINE

Starting Over With Your Attitude

I Thessalonians 5:9-11

The formula for successful TV news is weather, medical information, and drug busts. Everyone wants to know, "What's going down?" Who is winning the war on drugs?

The Drug Enforcement Agency reminds us that millions of Americans use cocaine. The cost of drug abuse is enormous. We know it in terms of dollars, crime, addicted babies, law enforcement, the courts, incarceration, and rehabilitation. Kilo by kilo, we are crumbling. We are caught in a war. In this rich nation, it is hard to believe that people find life so barren that they must blot it out with drugs.

In my city of Houston, we cannot afford to be smug. Cocaine streams north through Houston. As a major port city, it is a corridor to the empty souls of the American people.

Cocaine may be the most ruthless enemy we have ever faced. A war of words won't do it. It has to be a war of action.

What will control our destiny? It is our attitude. You and only you are responsible for your attitude. You choose your feelings, your behavior, and your attitude. You color your life with the thoughts you think. The ancient wisdom of the Old Testament book of Proverbs confirms that: "As you think in your heart, so are you." The Apostle Paul wrote to the sophisticates in Rome: "Be transformed by the renewal of your minds." Your mind runs twenty-four hours a day. No matter how you live, work, play or sleep, your mind is in gear. Ninety-three percent of your life is your thought life. Half of your health problems are attitudinal. The color of your thoughts color your life.

In the New Testament, the word "think" suggests an action of spreading out what is in your mind and taking inventory of it. You have seen street-hawkers who sell their wares from blankets. They spread their wares out for all to see. When you "think," you spread out your mental wares and take inventory. Paul commands, "Let this mind be in you which was also in Christ Jesus." Your mind is a wonderful gift. Your attitude is a function of your faith.

"We who lived in concentration camps," wrote Viktor Frankl, "can remember the men who walked through the huts comforting others, giving away their last piece of bread." They may have been few in numbers, but they offer sufficient proof that everything can be taken from a man but one thing: the last of the human freedoms to determine one's attitude in any given set of circumstances—to choose one's own way.

Olympic swimmer Mark Spitz put it bluntly, "You've got to get hungry if you want to prove something." Your attitude is a function of your faith.

In I Thessalonians chapter 5, Paul is addressing the issue of Christ's return to earth. The belief in an imminent return of Jesus Christ has stirred up all kinds of excitement within the Christian community in the port city of Thessalonica. They stopped going to school and doing their homework. They quit their jobs. They no longer mowed the lawn. They headed for the hammock and decided to wait for the return of Christ.

Through clenched teeth, Paul dictated something of his annoyance when he said, "You have no need to have anything written to you." Then, like a disgusted parent he said, "For you yourselves know well..." Which really means with hands on hips, "How many times do I have to tell you?" Tell them what? That the end of the world, the second coming of Christ, will be a surprise! It will be like a thief breaking and entering your home at night. They do not call ahead of time and give you a warning. It will be spontaneous. Unpredictable.

Numerous people in the church try to read prophetic signs. Purveyors of prophetic schemes flagrantly violate the Scriptures. They disobey God's word. Mark 13 records the words of Jesus, "Nobody knows the day or the hour...watch!" Your responsibility and mine is to avoid the arrogance of those who pretend to forecast the future. Palm readers, astrologers, and horoscopes are not part of God's redemptive program. We are to live the Christian life in light and sobriety. We are in a battle with evil. We are disciples of Christ. We are to be the salt, yeast, and light of the world. "Therefore encourage one another and build another up, just as you are doing." [I Thessalonians 5:11]

A good biblical word for our responsibility is "paraclete." A paraclete is one who comes along side for the other person's good. We are to be paracletes, not parasites. We are to be living stones as it suggests in I Peter 2:4, 5. We are to build up the temple of God. We are part of that temple.

On a hot summer night at the ballpark, a woman leaned over the railing and said to Yogi Berra, "You look exceptionally cool." Yogi trying to respond appropriately to the woman's comment said, "Thanks, ma'am, you don't look so hot yourself."

There is a world of difference between flattery and affirmation. Flattery is to manipulate through compliments. Affirmation is when you look at a person and not their achievements. You appreciate that person for who they are. Appreciation for being and not just doing is one of our responsibilities. Most of us are so goal-oriented and task-oriented that we cannot appreciate people for who they are.

During summer vacations, when our son Peter was in college, he worked as a volunteer at the Brookwood Community in Brookshire, Texas. Each Saturday, he would work from ten to four with functionally disabled adults. When it came to the end of the summer and his last Saturday, the members of the community decided to throw a party for Peter. They had cards which they had made, refreshments, and gifts. One of the gifts they presented to Peter was a chili dish with dividers in it in the shape of the state of Texas. The dividers kept the beans, rice and chili separate. The Brookwood Community molded and created this dish. These handicapped young adults mass-produced them along with many other items. At the end of the party, they presented Peter with a chili dish. A young resident proudly told Peter that he was the one that put the label that said, "Brookwood Community" on those dishes. To him, putting the label on was a mark of distinction and an indicator of his significance.

Attitude is more important than aptitude. Karl Menninger reminds us, "Attitudes are more important than facts."

Bill Higgs played soccer at the United States Military Academy at West Point. During a particularly tough game, Bill leaped for a head shot. Somehow, through a collision, he drove his elbow through his spleen. At the time, he did not know it. He simply knew that he was in great pain. He finished the remainder of the ball game by sheer determination.

As he left the playing field at West Point, he had six hundred feet to climb up to the dormitory. He felt bad. In fact, the steps became prohibitive for him. He knelt alone and prayed for strength. Finally, he made it up to the barracks. Somebody got him over to the hospital. He was too weak to make it on his own.

A surgeon happened to be checking on some rugby players in the hospital at West Point. He immediately diagnosed Bill's condition and declared him critical. They desperately needed blood. They literally went out to the streets of West Point and pleaded with people for AB+

blood to provide a transfusion. They operated to remove his spleen.

At 2 a.m., an orderly walked in to visit with Bill. He found him in the fetal position. The orderly recognized the gravity of his condition. He said, "Bill, are you a Christian?" Bill mumbled, "Yes." He asked, "Bill, do you know John 3:16?" Hesitantly, Bill repeated with him that much loved verse of Scripture. He patted him on the shoulder as to bid farewell.

At 6:30 a.m. that same morning, the soccer coach somehow slipped behind the barriers and visited at Bill's bedside. He tapped Bill on the shoulder and said, "Billy, they say you are going to be able to play soccer next year."

That was just the word that Bill needed to hear. It gave him hope. It changed his attitude. The attitude of the coach was contagious for Bill. The good news is that Bill lived to tell the tale. Indeed, he did play soccer that next year for West Point.

If you were asked to name five people who encouraged you in your life, I am certain one you would name would be a teacher. The role of the teacher often determines a student's attitude. Recently, I heard a geometry teacher tell the parents of her students, "Please don't tell your kids you couldn't do proofs either." Be careful what you tell a child. It can stick! It can determine a lifetime attitude.

How do you start over with your attitude?

Here are three suggestions:

1. Forgive! The Bible says, "Forgive one another as Christ has forgiven you." There is power in forgiveness. That is what the cross of Jesus Christ is all about. When

we refuse to forgive ourselves and others, we deny the cleansing power of the cross. Your immune system tells you that if you pour out negative thoughts, the endocrine system will empty those corrosive hormones into your life which generate malaise and chemical imbalance. But, when you pour thoughts of forgiveness into life, you tune your holistic being and radiance, strength, endurance, recovery, and energy head your way. Friend, rejoice! Christ has forgiven your sins. Repent. Claim God's power. Live as a forgiven person.

2. Forego! Forego the temptation to retaliate, to get even and to dwell on the destructive. It is so easy to soak up negatives. We can wallow in our pity. When you appreciate people, affirm people, love people and give yourself away, you forego the temptation to try to get even. Forego! Greet the wrong gesture with the right attitude.

Most of us will miss out on life's big prizes. Few of us can expect a Pulitzer, a Nobel, an Oscar, a Tony, an Emmy or a Heisman, but we are all eligible for life's little prizes: a pat on the back, a hug, a beautiful full moon on a fall night, a delicious meal prepared by a friend, and a glorious sunset.

3. Forge ahead! Your attitude is a function of your faith. I Thessalonians 5:11 reads, "Therefore encourage one another and build one another up, just as you were doing." What a superb piece of advice and affirmation. Come along side one another. We are in the construction business. We are living stones. Stones that make up the temple of God.

"You're an angel!" You have probably been told that more than once and did not believe it. If angels came in packages, we would probably pick the wrong one. Why? We are not sure what to look for in angels. Are they male? Are they female? Are they always naked, chubby cherubims? Or do they always look like something out of the Louvre? Do they look like the figures imposed on Christmas cards? Do they take the shape of Christmas tree ornaments?

Robots, androids, and extraterrestrials upstage angels today.

Angels show up on deserted highways when your car breaks down. Angels show up when you have a fall. Angles often are strangers. Angels often are rescuers. I like the wingless, flesh and blood kind of angels.

While skiing at Vail, I was standing in line with a friend at a chair lift. Two young children got on the chair just ahead of me. One did not get properly seated. He started to fall out of the chair. At best, he was probably seven years old. It took the chair supervisors several seconds to get it stopped. When they stopped the chair, young John was left hanging by one arm from the chair. He was crying out. Helplessness paralyzed all of us. Quickly, the chair attendants came to his aid. They ran with a ladder to try to reach him. However, he was just too far off the ground. He continued to hang on by just one arm. All of the crowd started to chant, "Hang on, John. Hang on, John!"

After several frustrating unsuccessful attempts to try to reach him, the chair attendants said, "Go ahead and fall, John. We will catch you."

John let go and at just the right moment, after the skis had sailed by him, the attendant caught John in a vice-like grip. It was an exciting moment. The lift

117

attendant was definitely an angel. His attitude made the difference. He forged ahead!

It was fascinating to hear the crowd respond. They all cheered. They cheered John and the attendant. As everyone filed by the attendant once the chair was back in operation, they congratulated him. He deserved the line, "You're an angel!"

To forge ahead has characterized numerous endeavors in the United States. Dr. Seuss had his first children's book rejected by twenty-three publishers. But the twenty-fourth publisher accepted it. He sold six million copies. *Green Eggs and Ham* has thrilled many children. The first year Coca-Cola went on the market, they sold only four hundred Cokes. In 1903, King Gillette produced the first safety razor. In the first year, King Gillette sold only fifty-one razors and one hundred sixty-one blades. But he chose to forge ahead. Louis Pasteur formulates the story of success in this statement that characterized his attitude, "My greatest strength lies solely in my tenacity."

Several years ago, a fascinating movie hit the summer market entitled "Dead Poet's Society." Throughout the movie, the characters used the phrase "Carpe Diem." It meant seize the day. Robin Williams played the role of a prep school teacher that pounded that phrase into the minds of his students. He did it in hopes they would be moved to capitalize on the great opportunities that life has to offer. He affirmed they could give themselves for a noble cause; that there was more to life than just materialism. So over and over, he drove that phrase home "Carpe Diem." Seize the day. For the Christian, our attitude ought to be different because of the forgiveness that Jesus Christ has extended to us. "Carpe Diem pro Christos!" That's the phrase I would like to use. "Seize the day for Christ!" Forgive. Forego. Forge ahead.

CHAPTER TEN

Starting Over
With Your Inferiority Complex

I John 4:4

Just ten years ago, there were 160 cities in the world with populations in excess of one million. When you name large cities, you cannot ignore Mexico City. To understand the overwhelming population of India, you must imagine that India has a dozen cities the size of Mexico City. By the year 2000, over 500 cities will exceed one million in population. It is not hard to imagine the whole world as one immense metropolis.

When you think of numbers like that, it is hard to imagine having your own identity. Do I count? Where do I fit in? Feelings of inferiority rush in. Despite sophisticated faces, we are all shrinking violets—shy, filled with self-doubt, and suffering inadequacy on occasion.

In 1899, Charles Duell was Commissioner of the United States Office of Patents. Duell urged President McKinley to abolish the patent office. Duell's logic was, "Everything that can be invented has been invented."

Starting Over With Your Inferiority Complex

Good thing McKinley did not listen to him. It would have been foolish to accept such a short-sighted recommendation. We would have missed out on our Ford F150 pick-ups, microwave ovens, VCRs, air conditioning, remote control, and cellular telephones.

Change is an absolute. Change is constant. Thank the Lord, God is not finished with us or the creation just yet.

We all need some stability zones in life. Home, work, and community. Community is the tough one. Maybe it is a softball team, a choir, a food pantry where you volunteer. It is the group within which you have identity outside of home and work.

When I was thirteen years old, Diana Gibbons invited me to a Sadie Hawkins party. Do you know what a Sadie Hawkins party is? It is where the girls invite the boys. She was as tall as I was. She wanted me to dance with her, but since she was a physically mature thirteen year old, I felt awkward. I was insecure. I had a rush of inferiority. I did dance with her, but it was not easy!

The trouble with an inferiority complex is that the right people never have it. No matter our age or stage in life, there are moments of self-doubt, "Maalox Moments," feelings of inferiority.

In the mind, you will find the rudiments of successfully beating that inferiority complex. There is a wonderful biblical principle found in Proverbs 23:7, "As you think in your heart, so are you." That is the source of the old adage: "You are what you think." What is down in the well will come up in the bucket. What is inside of you will always express itself. Think of yourself as inferior and you will upset your mental well-being which directly affects your physical well-being. We are psychosomatic people. Body, mind, and spirit constantly interact.

Is there such a thing as Christian conversion? Many people do not think so. Some would suggest that a conversion experience is only an esoteric psychological experience. Some would quickly put conversion in the category of hysterical reaction.

I am always uncomfortable with people who suggest that a Christian is someone who has been unhappily oriented in every area of life. Critics write off Christians as persons just bored and tired of mediocrity, or somebody off on a new emotional tangent. Some unfairly categorize converts to Christianity as social rejects—vulnerable and naive—someone who cannot keep up with the more aggressive superior specimens of the human race. Some have demeaned Christians as people who are struggling with an inferiority complex and desperately longing for superiority. Caught up in a web of intrigue, the Christian has been duped into a delusion of grandeur—a delusion of grandeur which links with some eternal omnipotent force. I disagree!

Caution! This psychological explanation is vulnerable. Any student of hysteria knows that its outgrowth is anger, deceit, depression, frustration, helplessness, megalomania, and narcissism. These stand in blatant contrast to the fruits of the Spirit which the Apostle Paul suggested: love, joy, peace, patience, kindness, goodness, faithfulness, gentleness, and self-control. If you prefer to use the term hysteria, you must at least admit that the hysteria of Christianity is different from any other form of hysterical reaction.

Again, in stark contrast, Christianity does not work this way. The experience of sins forgiven in Jesus Christ does not confuse people. On the contrary, use of logic, goals, talents and courage, which may have been blurred and foggy before, suddenly become clear and focused. People who were lost and leading lives heading nowhere suddenly are characterized by direction and purpose. You dare not explain Christian conversion on the basis of hysterical reaction. It is true that a conversion experience appears to be a psychological paradox because it is primarily a spiritual phenomenon with secondary psychological overtones. Psychology alone cannot give an adequate explanation of human reaction to the gospel of Jesus Christ. Conversion is more than an intellectual rearrangement of attitudes based on some external suggestion. Rather, something dynamic has happened to the personality. A conversion to faith in Jesus Christ means a new kind of generative mechanism has been introduced. Change is inevitable when that happens. The source for that change in the lives of those who profess faith in Jesus Christ is due to the work of the Holy Spirit.

Mark Twain was right! "Get the facts first. You can distort them later." Critics of Christian conversion need to get the facts first!

All of us, at some point, have encountered Gerber's baby food. Gerber's baby food came into existence out of a family need. Dan Gerber's wife forced him to strain a can of peas to experience what she had to put up with three times a day, seven days a week. Dan decided that there just had to be an easier way. He and his brother Frank owned a cannery. They were determined to find a solution. In 1928, they went to market with a line of five strained baby foods. Out of a family need, a personal need, they discovered a way to meet it.

How do you intend to confront your feelings of inferiority?

Here is a wonderful promise from I John 4:4, "The one who is in you is greater than the one who is in the world." You have a unique resource. You are not on your own. You are not totally left to your own devices. The source for the greatness in you is the Holy Spirit. God has promised that to you. Conscious of that unique power, I suggest the following ways of beating that inferiority complex.

1. You are a child of God. There is nothing inferior about that. You are able. You are competent. God has made you in his image. In your mind is a marvelous computer known as the brain. The brain has nerve cells called neurons. They breathe oxygen and give off carbon dioxide. Each has a life of its own. There are 10 billion to one trillion neurons in your brain. During pregnancy, they develop at a rate of 150 per second through nine months. No other creature has your brain power. Your brain power, plus the power of the Holy Spirit to those who are in Christ, is an unbeatable combination.

Paul Homer was a brilliant theologian at Yale Divinity School years ago. A presumptuous student once asked him why he believed in God. His profound reply was, "Because my mother told me." That is a simple start. But it is a start.

Harry Emerson Fosdick observed, "Religion begins when what God outwardly argued is inwardly experienced." "The one who is in you is greater than the one who is in the world." The power of the Holy Spirit, the spirit of God, is greater than the power of evil. The Holy Spirit is available to help you perceive something that is not otherwise perceivable. The amazing thing about the Holy Spirit is that it is self-authenticating. The Holy Spirit frees, convicts, disciplines, changes, and affirms. There is nothing inferior about that. You are a child of God.

2. You have the ability to cancel the negatives in your mind with positives. It is okay to talk to yourself. Have you ever noticed that the meanest things that we say, we say to ourselves? When you talk to yourself, maybe you should talk in terms of positives. William James taught that the greatest discovery of his era was that people can alter their lives by altering their attitudes. When you entertain negative thoughts about your ability, you invite destruction. You invite feelings of inferiority. The brain is competent to help you cancel it. You can cancel it with a positive thought about your ability. You can also cancel it with the knowledge that Christ loved you to the extent that he died for you.

The Los Angeles Times published a five-year study of the University of Chicago which focused on 120 of America's top artists, athletes, and scholars. "We expected to find tales of great natural gifts. We didn't find that at all. Their mothers often said it was their other child who had the greater gift."

What was the key element? For these successful people it was not talent, but extraordinary drive, determination, and commitment.

In 1970, Ali MacGraw told the world that love meant never having to say you're sorry. She made audiences

125

around that world weep at her tragic "Love Story" deathbed scene.

The devastating impact of early stardom, and the task of coping as that stardom slipped away, overwhelmed Ali. She became addicted to men and to alcohol. She has recently crawled out of that deep hole. She said, "I believe a lot of us feel a kind of hole in our heart. An unfocused ache that's fixed by some people eating too much. For others with freebase. In my case, I'm a romance junky."

She admitted herself to the Betty Ford Center. "I'm proof positive that you can work through stuff and with help—here comes the rest of my life!" She canceled the negatives and worked on her positives. You can, too.

George Bernard Shaw, the playwright, is featured each year in a festival at Niagara-on-the-Lake in Ontario. When Shaw was ninety years of age and close to death, he asked his nurse, "Dear, would you do me a favor? When the doctor comes in and says that I'm dead, would you ask for a second opinion?"

Maybe you need a second opinion on your condition. You may feel like you've had it. Maybe you have blown it! But remember, God loves you with a love that will not let you go. God's grace is always greater than our need.

Paul Tournier, the Swiss Christian psychologist said, "Perhaps that most powerful and unused gift of God is choice."

The New Yorker had a cartoon that featured the prodigal son, the father, and the neighbors all gathered in their splendor. The father is about to celebrate the return of the son. He is carving a huge roasted calf.

Suddenly, he turns to his son and with a wearied, worried look says, "Now, after all son, this is the fourth fatted calf."

Disraeli said, "Grief is the agony of an instant. The indulgence of grief is the blunder of time." You can cancel the negatives in your mind. God wants to give you a second opinion. You can come home again. The outstretched arms of the Savior reach for your embrace.

For many years, I have admired the Reverend Dr. Jim Glasse. He is a Presbyterian pastor. He has been the president of a seminary. He is a highly-regarded author. While greeting after worship one Sunday, I looked up and to my amazement, there was Jim Glasse. I wished him good morning and a "God bless you." I am insecure enough to wonder what Jim Glasse though of the service and the sermon. After all, he was a real professional; a man of standards and integrity. I also knew him to be a tough critic.

You cannot imagine the joy I felt when I read a note from Jim which arrived a few days later. In part, it said, "When I had a Sunday off, I decided to check in with you. But I got more than I bargained for! The spirit of the place and the style of your service broke through my professional shield. I was truly blessed by the whole experience and especially your sermon. You combined the prophetic and pastoral in a challenging, but non-threatening way." I learned from that and was blessed by it. That was a blessing for me. You can cancel the negatives. God has many more positives for you than any negatives you can conjure up.

3. Imaging is a gift. The psychological community talks about the gift of imaging. God has entrusted to us

the ability to image things. You can establish obstacles in your mind. But, you can also establish in your mind a positive image as to how you are going to handle a given situation. You can imagine what it is you must do and then do it well. Jonathan Winters, the comedian, quipped, "I couldn't wait for success, so I went ahead without it."

Have you ever observed a high jumper in the Olympics? The athlete, before approaching the crossbar, thinks through all of the action needed to clear the bar. The image is set in the mind. The athlete acts on the image.

Dr. Karl Menninger, of the Menninger Clinic in Topeka, Kansas, said that when you begin to see what you can become your problems are mostly over.

You cannot get well as long as the shackles of defeat trap you. If you are a prisoner of the past, you are a victim of your track record. When you do that, you deny the power of God's spirit. More than that, you deny the power of the resurrection of Jesus Christ. Forgiveness is God's gift for you.

Change begins at the place where you begin to dream holy dreams about what you can become. Abraham did it. Paul did it. Jesus did it. Life is shaped either by our dreams or by our problems. I have long been intrigued with Goethe's comments, "Tell me with whom you associated and I will tell you who you are."

Debbi Fields is the successful founder of "Mrs. Field's Cookies", Inc. She did not sell a single cookie the first morning she was in business. Instead, in frustration, she gave them out as free samples. That way, she kept her image intact. She imagined herself as a cookie entrepreneur. Today, she has a multimillion dollar cookie business. Imaging is a gift!

4. Fill your mind with affirmations from God. God will not protect you from negative thoughts. If you leave your doors unlocked, you welcome burglary and robbery. If you participate in a careless diet and ignore exercise, you are going to jeopardize your health. If you ignore the friends your children choose, then you are declining to nurture your child in the admonitions of the Lord.

God promised you, "I am with you always."

"God is our refuge and our strength, a very present help in time of trouble."

"No temptation will overtake you beyond that which can withstand."

"My grace is sufficient for you. My strength is made perfect in weakness."

Take time to pray over these affirmations. They are deserving of your reflection. They are a constant source of strength.

The great Reformed Swiss theologian Karl Barth wrote, "Communion with God is not a dash into security but a walk towards reality."

You can take the first step towards reality by affirming God's love for you. In the Old Testament, the word "faith" has a unique definition. It really means to put your full weight down on the faithfulness of God. Have you ever stepped out on a frozen pond and wondered whether the ice could sustain your weight? It is the kind of test to which God's word invites us. Go ahead! Put your full weight down on the faithfulness of God. Expect to be surprised!

Let's Start Over

The Holy Spirit is God's dynamic. It is God's power and presence. It is God's breath. It is not some vague, remote idea floating around in some theological mist. "He who is in you is greater than he who is in the world."

Dave Dravecky, the former San Francisco Giants pitcher, said, "God did not give me the cancer." Dave had a cancerous tumor removed from the deltoid muscle of his left bicep. That was his pitching arm. Doctors diagnosed him as desperately in need of surgery and substantial physical therapy that would be painful. His physician said, "You will never pitch again." Dravecky's faith in Jesus Christ was a constant source of strength for him. His physician was wrong. When Dravecky returned to pitch, he was getting dressed for his first start after his recovery. One of his teammates, Kevin Mitchell said, "It looks like Jaws took a bite out of you." The scar was severe on his left arm. His first night back, he beat the Cincinnati Reds 4-3. Dravecky went 8 innings and pitched a 4 hitter. It was a dramatic night. Roger Craig, the manager of the San Francisco Giants, said, "What we have here is nothing short of a miracle."

Since then, Dravecky has had his left arm and shoulder amputated. However, he continues to love life and face it courageously. Dave gives credit for his optimistic spirit to the Holy Spirit, God's dynamic—"He that is in you is greater than he that is in the world."

By God's grace, you can start over with your inferiority complex and beat it.

CHAPTER ELEVEN

Starting Over
With Your Prayer Life

Luke 11:9-13

My Firestones went bad! That was how I met Homer Potter. Homer Potter was the manager of a Firestone tire store. While I was receiving a new set of tires, I fell into conversation with Homer. He told me that he had many ministers among his regular customers. He told me how often he would say to these pastors, "Be sure and toss one off for me!" One day, he said it to a Pentecostal pastor. The Pentecostal preacher quickly turned to Homer and demanded, "Give me your hand!" With that, the pastor prayed! Homer said, "He prayed out loud, for everything and for everyone in the place; the tires, the tools and the trucks." It sobered the entire shop. Everything suddenly went quiet. Never again, he said, did he suggest to any pastor that he "toss one off for me!"

Traffic with the Almighty must never be treated casually. Prayer is part of that traffic with the Almighty.

131

It is communication with God. Personally, I am not opposed to auto-suggestion, psychic hygiene, primal screams, meditation, or jogging. But please don't confuse these things with prayer.

Often, we treat God as chief of the celestial fire department. We only cry out when we are in a panic. "Please God, help me now!" Then we want an immediate response. There is no time for reflection. It is a demand for a response. But I remind you, the Almighty is not on anybody's leash.

Gary Carter is a catcher with the Los Angeles Dodgers. Carter is a Christian. On his locker, he has a sign that reads: "With God, all things are possible." It is that attitude that we must bring to prayer.

Prayer is not a scheme! Neither is prayer a scream! Unfortunately, we often treat prayer as a scheme and a scream. What is prayer? Prayer is dialogue. Our dialogue with God is encouraged through Jesus Christ. When we are in right relationship with another person, it is easy for us to converse. At our house, dinner conversation flows easily when we are at peace with everyone present. That is true of our relationship with God. Through prayer, God invites us to a new dimension, to live beyond the level of survival. Try on this tough question: "Do you pray?" If the answer is yes, then allow me to push you further for another answer, "What do you pray for?"

Many people pray for the trivial—to find a lost wallet, to fix a broken automobile transmission, to find the proper washing machine repairman, to heal a marriage without counseling or to find a parking space in a crowded shopping center.

Dr. and Mrs. LeRoy Pesch have a gorgeous home overlooking the entire bay of Acapulco. Acapulco is one of the three major ports for Mexico. Not only is it a natural port, but also a haven for tourism. Surrounding that beautiful bay are some hills. At the 1,250 foot level, there is a stunning chapel with a dramatic cross towering over it. This white cross reaches some 128 feet towards the heavens. It is seen from every vantage point in the harbor.

The Pesch home lies in the shadow of the cross. Thus, the name "Casa En La Hombra De La Cruz."

We all walk under the shadow of the cross. God helps us to allow that shadow to fall across our every activity. If we walk in the consciousness of the shadow of the cross, we will do so more righteously and more deliberately. We will also pray with a greater sense of humility.

Tell me what it is you pray for and I will tell you what you really believe about God. Luke 11:9 reads, "I tell you, ask, and it will be given you; seek, and you will find; knock and it will be opened to you." That is not an invitation to turn God into a giant vending machine, a huge nuclear power plant, or a magnificently programmed computer floating somewhere out there in space. God is not just a fact for you to intellectualize, but one who claims our allegiance, our love, our relationships not the least of which is communication. To stay in proper relationship with my wife and children, I need to have an honesty session where I expose my feelings.

Many years ago, a young pastor helped me greatly through his conversational prayer. He did not scold. He did not use elitist language. He did not manipulate. He talked to God as a friend. In the moment he talked to God about my needs, I was touched. It was in that kind of atmosphere that I made a real commitment to Jesus Christ. That pastor's honesty, his comfortable style, and his compassion set a standard for my ministry.

A nine year old boy was helping his father clear some land. The young boy struggled with a heavy rock that was in his path. He could not budge that boulder. His father watched at a distance as the young boy strained to move the rock. Finally, the father asked, "Are you using all your strength?" Exasperated, the boy yelled, "Yes, I am!" Calmly, the father said, "No, you are not. You haven't asked me to help." When was the last time you really asked the Father to help you?

How do you characterize prayer? Prayer harmonizes your thoughts with the thoughts of God. It is an attempt to see everything as God's work; to confront each experience in a day as God's appointment. It is to submit every thought, wish, and resolve to God. It is to feel the sustaining everlasting arms about us. It is to sense that you are here on this planet on purpose and for a redemptive purpose.

"The time of business," wrote Brother Lawrence, "does not differ with me from the time of prayer; and in the voice and clatter of my kitchen, while several persons are at the same time calling for different things, I possess God in as great tranquility as if I were on my knees at the Blessed Sacrament."

If this is a materialistic world run by mechanical laws, then prayer is absurd! If that is your predilection, then prayer is unexplainable to the three pounds of grayish jelly which we call the brain. Dr. Paul Brand has performed over 10,000 surgical procedures on hands over forty years. His conclusion is, "I have never found a single technique to improve a normal, healthy hand." Take a look at your hand! In your hand are seventy muscles. There are thirteen hundred nerve endings per square inch on your finger tip. There are nineteen bones in the hand. The hand can lift a needle from a table. It can wrench the stubborn cap of an apple juice jar. It can communicate love to some significant other in your life by a gentle touch. It can be a deadly weapon when shaped into a fist. Did the hand develop accidentally or is it the result of some divine design?

In our high-tech age, robots intrigue us. Even the most sophisticated robot's sculpture is like a child's playdough creation compared with a Michelangelo masterpiece.

When we talk about prayer, we must acknowledge that reason has its limits. There are truths such as prayer which the brain can discover but never truly defend.

The Scripture invites us to, "Ask...seek...knock..." It also suggests, "We ought always to pray and not lose heart."

A number of years ago, Phil Donahue was working for CBS news. He got a scoop that there was a mine disaster. He was in the area. What a wonderful opportunity to get on national television! It was late and snow was falling. He confronted the anxious relatives and gathered around the feeble heat of a smelt pot at the mine. He listened as these humble people began to sing,

"What a friend we have in Jesus
All of our sins and griefs to bear
What a privilege to carry
Everything to God in prayer."

135

Then a local pastor prayed. Eloquence was not the pastor's strength but rather sincerity. Donahue said it was aesthetically beautiful and emotionally moving. It gave him goose bumps. But Donahue was frustrated. Because of the cold, the batteries that drove the TV camera were weak. He did not catch the singing and the prayer on camera. He knew it was good stuff for national television.

He explained his dilemma to the local pastor, that the camera wasn't working. He asked, "Would you go through your prayer again?" He explained there would be two hundred and fifty stations picking up the signal. That there would be millions waiting to hear his prayer. To the pastor's credit, he refused. He said, "I have already talked to God and to do it again would be wrong." Again, Donahue tried to persuade him. But the country preacher said, "No!" Donahue later referred to this man's response as a demonstration of moral courage. He said, "The man would not show biz for Jesus! He would not sell his soul for TV, not even for national TV, praise God, not even for CBS."

In America, where depression is more common than the flu, we need to discover the power of prayer. Prayer is therapeutic. Most people do not believe that prayer has a place in science. Yet, in a rigidly controlled scientific study on prayer, cardiologist Randolph Byrd, formerly a University of California professor, showed that prayer works. Prayer can be a powerful force in healing. Personally, I do not know how much credibility to give to this study. However, I find it fascinating. Here it is.

Starting Over With Your Prayer Life

During a ten month study, a computer assigned three hundred and ninety-three patients admitted to the coronary care unit at San Francisco General Hospital either to a group that was prayed for by home prayer groups (one hundred and ninety-two patients) or to a group that was not remembered (two hundred and one). The prayer groups were given the names of their patients, something of their condition, and were asked to pray each day, but were given no instruction on how to pray.

Allow me to share some of the results with you. They are striking! The "prayed for patients" differed from the others remarkably in several areas:

1. They were five times less likely than the unremembered group to require antibiotics.

2. They were three times less likely to develop pulmonary edema.

3. None of the prayed-for group required endotracheal intubulation, in which an artificial airway is inserted in the throat and attached to a mechanical ventilator.

4. Fewer patients in the prayed-for group died.

How do you assess that? Dr. William Nolan, who has written a book debunking faith healing, acknowledged, "Sounds like this study will stand up to scrutiny...maybe we doctors ought to be writing on our order sheets, 'Pray three times a day.' If it works, it works." (*Southern Medical Journal* 81:7, July 1988, pp. 826-829)

Every family has a character. In my family, there was "Uncle Dave." Uncle Dave had made a lot of money in the construction business. He did not smoke cigars, he chewed them. He drove the biggest navy blue Cadillac you could buy. In fact, he never drove it himself. He always hired someone else to do that. He would sit in the back seat with an ottoman at his feet and a large valise placed next to him that was alleged to have a substantial amount of cash in it. Several summers, I worked for Uncle Dave. He had a summer home north of Ottawa on the Ottawa River at a place called MacLarren's Landing. His beautiful log cabin summer home did not have running water or electricity. You had to go out back and pump from the well if you needed water. It was a good well. Neighbors used it. It was a community meeting place. Uncle Dave taught me many things. One of the things he taught me was the importance of priming the pump.

With the disciples, we cry out, "Lord, teach us to pray." Allow me to give you three practical suggestions for priming your prayer pump.

1. Be still. To become aware of the presence of God, we must slow down and assess our situation and our surroundings. In Psalm 46:10, the suggestion is made to us, "Be still and know that I am God." We need to experience calmness. We need to sense serenity. We need to let the peace of God wash over us. Could it be that posture makes a difference when we pray? I believe prayers can erupt from any physical position, but it does help to let the body relax, the mind clear, and the sense of a power beyond our own confront us. "To pray is to expose the shores of the mind to the incoming tide of the Holy Spirit." Rather than confronting God with voluminous speech, I suggest silence. Then you are ready to begin with prayers of thanks. Offer gratitude to God for all you are and have. Acknowledge the love extended

to you in Jesus Christ and the promised power of the Holy Spirit. Revel in it. Allow your mind to float freely in an attitude of thanksgiving. You are uniquely blessed!
2. Tear down the barriers. All of us carry excess mental baggage. There are differences which would deter us from sensing God's will: fears, resentments, jealousies, lusts, and hurts. All of us have knowledge, will, and emotions. Prayer is an act of the will. Before pleading your case before God, in the name of Christ, ask forgiveness for sins and resentments. There is a conditional aspect to prayer. In the prayer that Jesus taught his disciples, "Forgive us our debts as we forgive our debtors," that little word "as" makes a huge difference. The unconditional love of God in Jesus Christ is for you. Do not ever diminish the declaration from the cross, "Father, forgive them..."

Thomas Carlyle married shy, sensitive Jane. He was not particularly affectionate. At one point in frustration, Jane suggested to him perhaps a word of encouragement from him would not be misplaced. That was all it took for Carlyle's anger to burst into flames. "Woman, do you expect praise for doing your duty?" That demeaning response broke Jane's gentle spirit. She wilted physically and emotionally and eventually died. Her death brought enormous remorse to Carlyle. After her death he prayed, "Oh, God, if only I could have her back, even for five minutes, to tell her that I loved her through all that!" But, it was too late!

"If you write benefits in sand and injuries in marble you really do not want to pray." Tear down the barriers. The ball is in your court. What will you do about your estrangements?

139

Let's Start Over

God invites us to use our imagination. Imagination is a wonderful gift from God. Imagine God lifting the resentments we carry. We can imagine God reaching to the person who continually frustrates us and God's grace helping that person; helped in his mercy and healed by the power of his spirit. That is our prayer. God invites us to focus our prayers. Focus on your need and the need of others. All your concerns interest God. Even those thoughts that keep you awake at night intensely interest God.

In truth, we never successfully solve a problem until we correctly place the blame. All healing begins with a correct diagnosis. Time spent tearing down the barriers will open up new avenues to interface with God. If I understand intercession at all, it is loving your neighbor on your knees. Any barriers between you and God?

3. Listen. In the cacophony which surrounds us, it is difficult to listen. It is hard to for us to tune in to what God's will might be for us. It takes time to do that. C.S. Lewis prayed from 6-6:30 a.m. each day and whenever he had to wait!

Today, the National Basketball Association games are televised in seventy-five countries around the world. People tune in to see great basketball. If you want great things to happen in your prayer life, you must tune in. God does not measure effective prayer by how much we manage to get out of him, but how much of our lives we have turned over to God's management.

Archbishop Trench many years ago suggested, "We must not conceive of prayer as an overcoming of God's reluctance but as a laying hold of his highest willingness."

Starting Over With Your Prayer Life

You do not conclude your prayer when you open your eyes, get up off your knees, and unclasp your hands. Rather, prayer is everything you do.

Journalist Malcolm Muggeridge was working for the British Broadcasting Company when he stumbled upon Mother Teresa of Calcutta. As a skeptical reporter, he questioned the amount of time Mother Teresa and her Sisters of Mercy spent in prayers each day when they were daily deluged with human need. From Malcolm's vantage point, this was a waste of time.

His observation after several days amazed even him. His conclusion...somehow these nuns were able to accomplish more work after prayer. The two are linked; prayer and work, word and deed.

I am amazed at the number of times in my own ministry that a need has appeared—I pray about it and suddenly, the necessary gifts surface. Those surprising serendipitous moments are manifestations of the Holy Spirit. Our openness to God and our creativity are by design.

A warning is most appropriate: the Bible uses it over and over, "Hear, O Israel..." That means, listen! Be careful how you pray, you may be the answer. When Jesus prayed in Gethsemane, he was indeed the answer to his own prayer. An act of love is a prayer itself. Listen and believe God wants the very best for you. "If you then, who are evil, know how to give good gifts to your children, how much more will the Heavenly Father give the Holy Spirit to those who ask Him?" (Luke 11:13)

CHAPTER TWELVE

Starting Over With Your Time

Ephesians 5:15-17

On Thursday, July 5, 1990, the *Houston Chronicle* reported that Robert Lee "R.L." Blaffer II, died of an apparently self-inflicted gunshot wound to the head. R.L. was only 30 years old. He was a grandson of an Exxon founder and great-grandson of a Texaco founder. He was unemployed. Friends described him as a recluse. He was the heir to a huge fortune and possessed a large estate in his own name. What did he do with his time? He collected Mercedes automobiles.

That deeply saddened me. Here was a young man with everything that this world holds dear yet extremely despondent. Why did that story bother me so much?

Maybe it is because 40,000 children die every day on our planet. Two-thirds of them die from causes that are preventable. Vaccines, antibiotics, vitamins, clean water, and personnel to do the basic instructions in terms of hygiene could save many of these children. In the 1990's, we could cut that death toll of 40,000 children a day in half by an investment of approximately 2.5 billion dollars a year by the mid 90's.

Oh, but you say, that is a tremendous amount of money! You are correct. It is an enormous amount of money. However, it is what the United States tobacco companies spend on advertising in our country in one year. It is what the Russians spend on vodka in one month. It is less than what the world spends on armaments in one day.

To spend one's life buying Mercedes automobiles somehow does not add up to me. What an enormous waste of resources and time.

Only half the children in the developing world have access to clean drinking water and fewer have access to sanitary waste disposal facilities. Nearly one hundred million children of primary school age are not taking part in any education program. In the United States, one out of four children is born into welfare. One third of our teenagers will drop out of high school. Dropouts do not get steady work until age twenty-six.

The Bible has a great word of advice for all of us in this matter of reckoning with our time. There are some things we can do with the time we are allotted. With the time we are given, there are some things we must do. The New Testament expresses this in a curious word found in the Epistles of Paul. In Ephesians chapter Five, the Apostle Paul writes, "Look carefully then how you walk, not as unwise men but as wise, making the most of the time, because the days are evil." Other versions use the phrase, "Redeeming the time."

Let's Start Over

The Christian belief is that Christ came to redeem the world. The metaphor was taken from the practice of liberating slaves. They were "bought back", liberated, set free but at a price. Paul suggests that all of us are not automatically on the good side of the Kingdom. There is nothing in the passage of time that will lift us up. Going downhill is so much easier. That is why Paul uses the metaphor. "The times are evil," says the Apostle. That is not just a passing remark about the conditions in Ephesians about the middle of the first century. He is going deeper. Time may be against us in our struggle to be God's people. But time can be redeemed. Every event in time, no matter how heart-breaking, can be redeemed and the Apostle's advice is to do just that.

"Don't stop to look at anything or we won't have time to see everything." That comment was made by a tourist to a friend upon entering a museum.

Time is life! Time is irreversible. Time is irreplaceable. To waste your time is to refuse to master your life. Queen Elizabeth I, in 1603, said with her dying breath, "All my possessions for a moment of time."

Somehow, we feel we can save ourselves if we will just get better organized. If only we could go to a time-management seminar and then straighten everything out. Then, somehow, our lives would be easier. That strums every chord of guilt in anyone even moderately imbued with the good old American work ethic.

For all of us, time that once seemed free, flexible and elastic has grown tight and elusive, and so our measure of its worth is dramatically changed. In Florida, a man billed his ophthalmologist ninety dollars for keeping him waiting an hour. In California, a woman hires "a personal shopper" to go shopping for her, out of a catalog! You can have a fax machine in your car for $1,500. Pollster Louis Harris concluded, "Time may have become the most precious commodity in the land." We are swamped. We need help.

Today, the average work week including commuting is 47 hours. In some professions, that amount is often stretched to an 80 hour work week. Vacations have been shortened to the point where they are frequently no more than long weekends. And the Sabbath is for—what else—? Shopping!

Will Durant, the ubiquitous historian, once observed that "no man who is in a hurry is quite civilized." Time does bestow value. In our culture, we are at the breaking point as far as the family is concerned. Every relationship of value demands time. Many people are so obsessive-compulsive that they start the day with a list of eleven things to do and end up going home for the evening with a list of fourteen items to do including the original eleven.

The drill for time management is well known:

1. Establish goals and put them in writing.
2. Prioritize the goals according to realistic deadlines.
3. Review the goals periodically.
4. Block healthy hunks of time for reflection and physical conditioning.
5. Avoid interruptions.

I wish I could say that I faithfully do that. I wish life was that simple for me. It is not. Pastors cannot put people in crisis on hold. A response is needed and demanded. Time is often my personal enemy. I schedule carefully. I organize consistently. But interruptions are part of my calling. A pastor empathizes with people in a variety of emotional states. Often, we are present when someone's feelings soar to the peaks of ecstasy or plunge to the depths of despair. What a privilege!

One Wednesday, I had one of those emotional roller coaster days. At 1 p.m., I had a graveside service for an infant. Ellie and Phil's child was stillborn. I had not met them. They resided in Dallas. Phil's great-grandmother was a member of my congregation. That was my only connection.

The children's area of a cemetery makes me more sensitive. It was a dreary day in January. Poinsettias, toys, and Christmas ornaments marked the headstones. You did not need an imagination to visualize some of the pain connected to these losses.

As I approached the young couple standing alone under the canvas covering, I saw the mother touch the tiny white casket. The pink roses were beautiful. But nothing could mask the pain. My heart ached for them. Only the funeral director and the great-grandmother stood to the side. As I walked towards them, the funeral director greeted me and encouraged me to comfort them. That was unusual. Funeral directors are familiar with the dynamics of grief and, because of repeated experiences, all too used to them. And yet, even he was touched with the pathos of this situation.

I introduced myself and attempted to comfort them. I prayed for them. I prayed with them. I tried not to be formal, but to relate the hope that has its source in Jesus Christ. Though strangers to me, they invited me into their feelings in unique fashion. It was not just difficult to walk away with them from the burial site, it was difficult to control my own emotions.

Later that same day, hugging, jumping, laughing and crying, Charlie and Cheryl yelled out their "good news" to me. The adoption agency had just called at 5 p.m. that evening. The good news was that they could pick up their son in Austin the next day. Talk about the peak of ecstasy. I was privileged to be there with them. What a thrill! They could hardly control their emotions. Again, it was difficult to control my own tears. This time, tears of joy. Why should I? I love what I am doing. I am privileged. I am thankful that God has called me to this unique emotional roller coaster called pastoral care.

"It is ironic," writes social theorist Jeremy Rifkin in *Time Wars*, "that in a culture so committed to saving time we feel increasingly deprived of the very thing we value." People do feel more harried by their life-styles. Peoples' schedules are more ambitious. There is just not enough time to fit in all the things we feel have to be done. If you live what actuaries call a "normal life," you will spend five years of your life standing in line and two years trying to return phone calls!

The question is, whose schedule are we reading? Ours or God's? Is it possible for the two to be complementary?

I often ask people if they are having any fun. Often, the answer is, "I don't know!" We now have phones in our cars, laptops on our flights, and the humming fax machines bringing us more junk.

One man said, "People are so crazy now that they call to tell you your fax line is busy."

Let's Start Over

One of the sad characteristics of our day is that we are contracting out for family care. If you contract out everything, including family care, you have an enterprise, not a family! The home no longer is your sanctuary. It then becomes a benign environment in which one recuperates from problems at work.

Listen to what people say: "Tired is my middle name." "You are addicted to overwork!" The question is, where is there time for development of wholeness? Where is the time to enhance spiritual enlightenment?

How does a child spell l-o-v-e? The child spells love, t-i-m-e!

As parents, we want our children to know us as something other than just providers. Claire Booth Luce was in the United States House of Representatives as a Republican from Connecticut. She was an American playwright. Brilliant, ebullient, at age 75 she was asked, "Do you have any regrets?" Her response: "Yes, 56 years ago one of my girlfriends had a brain tumor. She asked me to come visit her three times before she died. I never did! I was always too busy. Couldn't take the time. When the news came that she had died, I was totally chagrined...humiliated...mortified. That is one of my regrets."

Relationships take time. For an acquaintance to become a friend, time is involved. The Spaniard, Francisco Pizarro, sailed to South America in 1502. This battle-hardened veteran was convinced that a rich empire lay to the south. He drew his sword and dug a line in the black, pebbly sand of Isla Del Gallo. He challenged his men to cross that line and follow him.

Starting Over With Your Time

"Comrades and friends," he shouted, "there lies the part that represents death, hardship, hunger, nakedness, rains and abandonment. This side represents comfort. Here you return to Panama to be poor; there you may go on to Peru to be rich. Choose which best becomes you as good Spaniards!"

Thirteen men crossed the line. Without remorse, they did discover wealth by overthrowing the Incas and stealing the gold and silver of Peru.

Sometimes a line has to be drawn. Where are you willing to draw the line with your time?

There are 10,080 minutes ahead of you this week. How do you intend to use them? Oh you may feel that you are fully self-reliant. That may well be the case. Self-reliance is a valuable commodity. I celebrate it. It is woven into the fabric of the American dream. But you can carry self-reliance so far that it not only makes people strong, it makes them hard and cynical.

Dr. Roy Menninger, of the famed Menninger Clinic in Topeka, Kansas, deplored the "I must always be strong" syndrome of American men. He went on to say, "The American male sees himself as a very high-powered piece of machinery rather than as a human need system." We are vulnerable. To admit our dependency and our feebleness is not to demean our humanity. To admit to a family member or a friend, "I need you," may be the beginning of help.

A very intelligent mother was asked what she would like to give her children as an inheritance. Her reply, "There are two lasting things I would like to give my kids. One of these is roots; the other is wings. The first is easier than the second."

Let's Start Over

Most of us struggle with a frantic pace. Our frazzled schedule leaves little room for walking on the beach, playing on the carpet with children or grandchildren, teaching a Sunday School class, eating dinner by candlelight, finding solace through a family member or a friend. If you consistently choose work over these alternatives, you really do have a problem managing time.

In the midst of our numbness of overextended vulnerability, we leave ourselves unaware of, if not callous to, the abundant life God promises to us in Jesus Christ.

Composer Franz Schubert said, "I'd rather lead a life of uncer-tainty and poverty than one of drudgery."

How does that strike you? Are you spending your life in drudgery? Maybe you need to take a vacation from drudgery. Try gliding along on a cloud of carefree whimsy some Monday through Friday. A few rounds of miniature golf may well be more important for you than additional meetings.

At Grace Presbyterian Church, I have a DWI. It does not mean "Driving While Intoxicated" but rather, "Dave Wants It." What is it that I want? I want one hour meetings. That is a DWI. It is not unusual over the course of a year for me to participate in 350 meetings. My calendar sadly shows it. I expect one hour meetings. I cannot afford to attend meetings that have no termination point. When you tell people up front that at the end of the hour, they can leave and they can expect that I will leave, it is amazing how much we can accomplish in that period of time. If the committee sets no adjournment time, it is amazing how much time can evaporate.

John F. Welch, Jr., president of General Electric Company, is regarded as one of the most successful CEOs in America. He recently made a decision. He goes home every evening at 6 p.m. He encourages his staff to follow his example. Part of what he has said about the management of time is important to his employees at General Electric. He wants them to spend more time with their families and to be rounded, whole people. People seldom harvest creativity out of exhaustion. The good news is, Welch does not just talk about it, he does it. When you get someone like the president of General Electric talking like that, you know you have a tremendous change in values about the work place.

The question that demands a response from all of us is, "Are we redeeming the time?"

It is all too probable that your schedule leaves no opportunity to fulfill the Psalmist's suggestion, "Be still and know that I am God."

Frankly, there is little in life that can bump that from the top of our priority list.